WILL SMITH

Recent Titles in Greenwood Biographies

WILL SMITH

A Biography

Lisa M. Iannucci

GREENWOOD BIOGRAPHIES

GREENWOOD PRESS
An Imprint of ABC-CLIO, LLC

A B C 🟢 C L I O

Santa Barbara, California • Denver, Colorado • Oxford, England

Library of Congress Cataloging-in-Publication Data

Iannucci, Lisa.
   Will Smith : a biography / Lisa M. Iannucci.
      p. cm. — (Greenwood biographies)
   Includes bibliographical references and index.
      ISBN 978-0-313-37610-8 (hard copy : alk. paper) — ISBN 978-0-313-37611-5
(ebook) 1. Smith, Will, 1968– 2. Actors—United States—Biography.
3. African American actors—Biography. 4. Rap musicians—United States—
Biography. I. Title.
   PN2287.S612I23   2010
   791.4302'8092—dc22   2009028798
   [B]

14   13   12   11   10   1   2   3   4   5

This book is also available on the World Wide Web as an eBook.

Visit www.abc-clio.com for details.

ABC-CLIO, LLC
130 Cremona Drive, P.O. Box 1911
Santa Barbara, California 93116-1911

This book is printed on acid-free paper ∞
Manufactured in the United States of America

CONTENTS

Photo essay follows page 78

SERIES FOREWORD

In response to high school and public library needs, Greenwood developed this distinguished series of full-length biographies specifically for student use. Prepared by field experts and professionals, these engaging biographies are tailored for high school students who need challenging yet accessible biographies. Ideal for secondary school assignments, the length, format and subject areas are designed to meet educators' requirements and students' interests.

Greenwood offers an extensive selection of biographies spanning all curriculum related subject areas including social studies, the sciences, literature and the arts, history and politics, as well as popular culture, covering public figures and famous personalities from all time periods and backgrounds, both historic and contemporary, who have made an impact on American and/or world culture. Greenwood biographies were chosen based on comprehensive feedback from librarians and educators. Consideration was given to both curriculum relevance and inherent interest. The result is an intriguing mix of the well known and the unexpected, the saints and sinners from long-ago history and contemporary pop culture. Readers will find a wide array of subject choices from fascinating crime figures like Al Capone to inspiring pioneers like

Margaret Mead, from the greatest minds of our time like Stephen Hawking to the most amazing success stories of our day like J. K. Rowling.

While the emphasis is on fact, not glorification, the books are meant to be fun to read. Each volume provides in-depth information about the subject's life from birth through childhood, the teen years, and adulthood. A thorough account relates family background and education, traces personal and professional influences, and explores struggles, accomplishments, and contributions. A timeline highlights the most significant life events against a historical perspective. Bibliographies supplement the reference value of each volume.

ACKNOWLEDGMENTS

Some books can be tedious to write and some are just plain ol' fun. As a fan of Will Smith's from his beginning rap days all the way through his latest hit movies, I have thoroughly enjoyed writing this book. Will Smith is pure entertainment. So thanks, Will, for making this book so easy to write; I'm eager to see what's next! I'd also like to thank my editor, George Butler, for his patience and guidance and Kristi Ward for trusting me with such a great topic. And, finally, I'd like to thank those who contributed to this book, including the experts who provided their opinions on Will's success and his acting coach, Aaron Speiser, who graciously shared some insight as to how Will has become such a fascinating actor to watch. And, of course, I can't do any of this without my great family— Nicole, Travis, Samantha, and my mom, Patricia Quaglieri. Love you!

INTRODUCTION

In 1975, Will Smith was only seven years old when Americans bought their movie tickets, popcorn, and soda and sat down in the theaters to watch *Jaws*, a psychological thriller about a great white shark who was attacking beachgoers in Amity Island, a fictional resort town. The movie was directed by Steven Spielberg, who at the time was a television director who had previously directed only a few movies before this feature hit the screen. The movie starred actors Roy Scheider and Richard Dreyfuss.

When *Jaws* was released on June 20, 1975, it opened at 465 theaters and became one of the first blockbuster movies. What is a blockbuster movie? It's a movie that costs a lot of money to make, is typically cast with big-name stars, and shines at the box office, often setting records and bringing in much more than it cost to make.

Jaws did just that. It grossed more than $7 million that weekend and was the top grosser for the following five weeks. It eventually grossed more than $470 million worldwide and was the highest grossing box-office film until *Star Wars* debuted two years later, also a Spielberg production. The movie, however, wasn't a success because it starred Roy

Scheider and Richard Dreyfuss, although they were great in the movie. Moviegoers flocked to see the movie because of its action-packed plotline and special effects.

Other movies, such as *The Omen, Wall Street*, and *Star Wars*, also became blockbusters in the summers to follow. Even movies of earlier years, such as *Gone with the Wind* (which made $400 million), were considered blockbusters of their time, but the term wasn't quite as popular until the 1970s. Interestingly, these movies, and others since, have one thing in common—great plotlines and special effects.

Will Smith was just a young boy when these movies were breaking records and making millions for the Hollywood industry—he might even haven been in the audience with his brother and sisters. Little did he know then that his name would, one day, become synonymous with the term *summer blockbuster* and that his movies would set even bigger box-office records than these movies had.

After becoming a successful rapper and sitcom star and before turning his attention to becoming a movie actor, Will and his agent first sat down and dissected the blockbuster movies. He wanted to know what the formula was for a successful blockbuster movie, and he and his agent soon realized that successful movies included action, special effects, and, in most cases, villains. Will decided that this was the formula he would stick to in order to become a success.

And he did just that with movies such as *Men in Black* and *Independence Day*, which were monumentally successful. Along the way, Will also chose movies that would stretch him as an actor, but when those movies didn't live up to expectations (e.g., *Wild, Wild West*), Will returned to his guaranteed formula. Interestingly, though, a funny thing happened on the way to the blockbuster movie, something that Will perhaps didn't count on.

Moviegoers, who often choose movies based on plotline alone, were now picking movies simply because they were associated with the name Will Smith. Will's name associated with a summer movie was almost a guaranteed success. Fans didn't care what the movie was about; they would go see it just because Will was in it. He's called the "king of Hollywood" and "the summer blockbuster champ," and it's said that he owns the Fourth of July movie weekend, setting incredible box office records that weekend alone over the past few years.

People were going to see a Will Smith movie, not a movie that just happened to star Will Smith. People would buy tickets just because they wanted to see what he would do next. Online bloggers have even joked about how Will could save just about any movie, regardless of the premise. People didn't go see *Jaws* because of Roy Scheider, and they didn't go see *Star Wars* because of Harrison Ford—they went because of the plot-line. In the beginning of Will's career, people would see his movies because they looked good, and although that's still true today, most people just say, "It's a Will Smith movie; it's going to be good." He's the biggest box-office draw in Hollywood by name alone.

In addition to his Hollywood success, Will has also become known as the nice guy in Hollywood. Everybody seems to like him—old, young, male, and female. He crosses all racial and cultural barriers—he's known around the world in every country. Some have said that he's the most recognizable man on the planet. The Daily Mind, an online blog, says that Will has charisma; he makes anyone he talks to feel like they are funny and empowers people to write their own rags to riches story.[1] The blog also said that Will listens well, which you can see when he's doing television interviews; he enjoys the stories the talk-show hosts share just as much as he enjoys sharing his own.

Will also seems to be a what-you-see-is-what-you-get type of person. Even in his relationship with actress Jada Pinkett, there have been few surprises. He seems as loving and caring in that relationship as he does to his fans and movie audiences.

Looking back, nobody thought that this young, middle-class rapper from Philadelphia would hit it this big. Will has achieved what no other person in Hollywood has been able to accomplish to his extent. He's achieved success in music, television, and movies. He's recognizable, setting box-office records. Hollywood knows that if a movie is a Will Smith movie, it's most likely going to be successful.

Will's life story is fun to read. He's the type of person who never gives up no matter what obstacles he faces—and he's faced a few throughout his career. He's definitely someone that can motivate and encourage others to succeed as well. He's funny and a delight to watch when he performs.

Reading Will's story should leave you eager to see what he's going to do next. No longer in his twenties, he's not sure how many more action movies he has in him, so he's choosing deeper, more thought-provoking films (e.g., *Seven Pounds*), and audiences are adapting to a new Will. He's taking his success behind the camera with his production company, and he's also tutoring his young children as they enter the realm of show business. There's no stopping Will and whatever he wants to do. Stay tuned, because his story isn't done being written.

NOTE

1. "I Am Charisma: Developing Charisma Like Will Smith." *The Daily Mind.* http://www.thedailymind.com/how-to/i-am-charisma-developing-charisma-like-will-smith.

TIMELINE: EVENTS IN THE LIFE OF WILL SMITH

September 25, 1968   Willard Christopher Smith Jr. is born in Wynnefield, Pennsylvania—the second child to Willard Christopher and Caroline Smith. His other sibling, sister Pamela, was born four years earlier.

1971   Twin siblings Harry and Ellen are born.

1979   Sugarhill Gang's "Rapper's Delight" is released. Will starts writing rap songs.

1985   Will meets Jeffrey "DJ Jazzy Jeff" Townes and forges partnership and friendship.

July 26, 1986   DJ Jazzy Jeff and the Fresh Prince sign a record contract with Word-Up Records Enterprises Inc.

1986   DJ Jazzy Jeff and the Fresh Prince release their first single, "Girl's Ain't Nothin' but Trouble." It reaches #81 on the R&B charts.

March 1987   First album, *Rock the House*, debuts on Jive Records and sells more than half a million albums.

1988   The duo releases their second album, *He's the DJ, I'm the Rapper*, which becomes rap music's first double-vinyl LP release.

1989	*Parents Just Don't Understand* wins 1989 Grammy Award for Best Rap Performance, the first Grammy Award ever to be given out for rap.
1989	The IRS confiscates all of Will's possessions to repay debt after he fails to pay taxes on millions he earned.
1989	Releases the album *And in This Corner*.
1990	Earns a role on NBC's *The Fresh Prince of Bel-Air*.
1990	Will dates young actress Sheree Elizabeth Zampino.
1991	Releases the album *Homebase*.
December 24, 1991	Will proposes to Zampino.
May 9, 1992	Will marries Sheree Zampino.
1992	Earns role in *Where the Day Takes You*.
November 11, 1992	First son, Willard Christopher "Trey" Smith III, is born.
1993	Will is nominated for a Golden Globe Award for Best Performance by an Actor in a TV-Series—Comedy/Musical.
1993	Will stars in *Made in America*.
1993	Earns rave reviews as Paul in *Six Degrees of Separation*.
October 12, 1993	Releases *Code Red*, the fifth album by the Fresh Prince and DJ Jazzy Jeff.
1994	Will is nominated for a Golden Globe for Best Performance by an Actor in a TV-Series—Comedy/Musical.
1994	Wins ASCAP award for role on *The Fresh Prince of Bel-Air*.
February 1, 1995	*He's the DJ, I'm the Rapper* is certified by the Recording Industry Association of America (RIAA) as three-times platinum.
1995	Will divorces Zampino. Zampino gets reported $900,000 lump sum settlement plus $24,000 per month in alimony and child support for Trey.
April 7, 1995	Release of *Bad Boys*, for which Will earns $2 million. Movie earns $141 million worldwide.

1995	Starts dating actress Jada Pinkett.
1996	*The Fresh Prince of Bel-Air* ends its six-year run.
July 3, 1996	Release of the movie *Independence Day*, which earns $816 million worldwide.
1997	Does voice-over for *Happily Ever After's Pinocchio*.
July 2, 1997	*Men in Black* is released, for which Will earns $5 million. Movie earns $587 million worldwide.
November 25, 1997	Releases *Big Willie Style*, his first solo album.
December 31, 1997	Marries Jada Pinkett.
1998	Will is named one of *People* magazine's 50 Most Beautiful People.
1998	Will is founder of Overbrook Entertainment, named after his high school in Philadelphia, Pennsylvania.
July 9, 1998	Will and Jada's son, Jaden Christopher Syre Smith, is born
November 1998	Release of *Enemy of the State*, for which Will earns $14 million. Movie earns $250 million worldwide.
1999	Wins Grammy Award in 1999 for best rap solo performance ("Gettin' Jiggy Wit It!")
July 1999	Release of *Wild, Wild West*, for which Will earns $7 million. Movie earns $222 million worldwide and is considered a box-office flop.
1999	Releases the album *Willenium*.
October 31, 2000	Will and Jada's daughter, Willow Camille Reign Smith, is born.
November 2000	Release of *The Legend of Bagger Vance*. Movie earns $38 million worldwide.
April 2001	Will's first book, *Just the Two of Us*, is published.
December 25, 2001	Release of *Ali*. Will earns a $20 million paycheck, which makes him part of the A-list. Movie earns $87 million worldwide.
February 12, 2002	Will learns he is nominated for an Academy Award for *Ali*.
July 3, 2002	Release of *Men in Black II*, for which Will earns $20 million. Movie earns $441 million worldwide.

July 18, 2003   Release of *Bad Boys II*, which earns $273 million worldwide.

2003   Premiere of *All of Us* sitcom on UPN network.

2004   Release of *I, Robot*, for which Will earns $28 million. Movie earns $345 million worldwide.

2004   Will does voice-over in the animated film *Shark Tale*. Movie earns $367 million worldwide.

February 11, 2005   Release of *Hitch*. Movie earns $368 million worldwide.

2005   Releases *Lost and Found* album.

2006   Release of *The Pursuit of Happyness*, for which Will earns $10 million. Movie earns $304 million worldwide.

February 25, 2007   Will is nominated for his second Academy Award, for *The Pursuit of Happyness*.

2007   Release of *I Am Legend*, for which Will earns $20 million. Movie opens to $77 million weekend and makes total worldwide earnings of more than $585 million.

2008   Release of *Hancock*. Movie earns more than $107 million.

2008   Release of *Seven Pounds*. Movie earns more than $167 million

Chapter 1

EARLY LIFE: A PRINCE IS BORN

It's March 24, 2002, and 33-year-old Will Smith sits in the Kodak Theater in Hollywood, California, flanked by his wife Jada Pinkett Smith. The *74th Annual Academy Awards* show—more commonly known as the Oscars—is underway. The coveted Oscars are awards of merit for members of the film industry and are presented annually by the Academy of Motion Picture Arts and Sciences. Will Smith is anxiously waiting to find out if he's won Best Actor in a Leading Role for his portrayal of the legendary boxer Muhammad Ali in the 2001 film *Ali*.

Will's competitors for this best actor award were veteran actors who had, by that point in their careers, made a solid impact on the film industry. There was Denzel Washington, who played Alonzo Harris, a police narcotics officer in *Training Day*. Washington is a critically acclaimed actor who had previously been nominated for, and won, several Academy Awards, including one for his portrayal of Malcolm X in the movie *Malcolm X* a decade earlier. Russell Crowe portrayed John Forbes Nash in *A Beautiful Mind* and is also a multiple Academy Award nominee. Sean Penn portrayed a mentally retarded man who fights for custody of his daughter in *I Am Sam*. Penn has also been nominated for previous Oscar awards. Tom Wilkinson, another newbie of the bunch, was also up for his first nomination for his role as Matt Fowler in the movie *In the Bedroom*. Wilkinson had also been honored with multiple other film award nominations.

Until this point in his career, Will had been more of an action-movie star, shining in blockbusters such as *Men in Black* (1997), which grossed $587 million worldwide, and in the 1995 action comedy *Bad Boys*, which brought in $140 million worldwide. In between these successful flicks, Will starred in the megablockbuster *Independence Day*, which tore up the 1996 Fourth of July box office and brought in $811 million worldwide.

However, Will's role as Muhammad Ali was different. Yes, the movie was filled with real-life boxing action, but it was nothing like the previous special-effects movies in which he had starred. Instead, it was jam-packed with drama and emotion, which allowed Will to expand and show off his acting range. It was this role that allowed Will, who had come to Hollywood only a little more than a decade earlier as a young teen rapper, to show that he deserved to be in the same category as Washington, Crowe, and the others.

Portraying Muhammad Ali was the most dramatic role Will had undertaken at that point in his career, and he threw himself into it. He gained 35 pounds of pure muscle and trained for a year by running, jumping rope, sparring, and weight training.[1] During the filming, Will wanted to make the role as realistic as possible, so he took punches to the face. Hollywood recognized the hard work, emotion, and dedication that Will brought to the role and awarded him the nomination for best actor. Although Denzel Washington took home the Oscar that night, Will took a huge step forward in his movie career—Hollywood was taking him seriously.

Will didn't wallow in self-pity about his loss. Instead, he wanted, and needed, to know what he had to do to improve himself, to make himself as good an actor as Washington. So, for the first time in his career, he hired an acting coach. He wanted to become an even better actor, and when Will Smith sets out to do something, he does it.

Perhaps Will's hard work and dedication are genetic. Will, who was born Willard C. Smith II on September 25, 1968, is the second child to father Willard Smith Sr. and mother Caroline. His older sister, Pamela, was born in 1964. Will was born and raised in West Philadelphia in a town called Wynnefield. Wynnefield, also known as "The Field," was, at this time, an upscale and predominately Jewish American community. It was also considered a safe town with local boutiques and high-end stores.[2]

It was the 1960s when Will came into the world, and so much was happening. It was during this decade that John F. Kennedy took office as the 35th president of the United States. The civil rights movement to abolish racial discrimination against African Americans was underway, and protests took place all over the country. Human rights icons Martin Luther King Jr. and Malcolm X preached and led the way for African Americans to obtain equal rights and freedom. In 1963, Martin Luther King Jr. delivered his historic "I have a dream" speech in Washington, D.C. The Civil Rights Act was signed in 1964. It was also the decade when women began fighting for their rights, led by women's rights advocates Betty Friedan and Gloria Steinem.

The 1960s was coined the decade of sex, drugs, and rock and roll in American culture. It was the era of the hippies and the infamous Woodstock Music Festival, which interestingly took place in Bethel, New York, not Woodstock, New York, and was held in 1969. The sounds of the music industry were rapidly changing as Berry Gordy Jr. founded Motown Records; the Beatles invaded America; and music legends Jimi Hendrix, Bob Dylan, the Rolling Stones, Pink Floyd, and the Beach Boys were fast becoming some of the most popular acts of the decade. In the sports world, Muhammad Ali—then known as Cassius Clay—was just at the beginning of what would become a long, illustrious boxing career. Known for his "float like a butterfly, sting like a bee" persona, he earned a perfect record of 19-0, with 15 knockouts from 1960 to 1963.

In the film industry, African American actors were mostly used as uneducated nannies and servants, gangsters, pimps, and prostitutes, although that started to change in the late 1960s and 1970s when they were given roles as police officers. Except for a few exceptions, such as the legendary actor Sidney Poitier, blacks were not offered any lead roles. Poitier had a few standout performances, including his roles in *To Sir with Love* and *In the Heat of the Night*. Other films such as *To Kill a Mockingbird* and *The Pawnbroker* focused on the civil rights movement. Another black actor and singer, Harry Belafonte, was a major supporter of the civil rights movement and considered one of Martin Luther King Jr.'s confidants, supporting him financially during his preaching days.

Unfortunately, the 1960s were marked by turbulent events. In 1960, escalating racial tensions lead to riots in Los Angeles, California, and, in 1969, more racially motivated riots took place in Harlem, New York, and Philadelphia, Pennsylvania. Sadly, during the 1960s, President Kennedy, Martin Luther King Jr., and Malcolm X were assassinated.

Back home in West Philadelphia, however, Will's parents continued to work hard to give their children a good life and happy home. They wanted to teach their children the value of respect and hard work.

Will's father owned a refrigeration business, called Arcac.[3] His mother, Caroline, graduated from Carnegie Mellon and worked for the Philadelphia School District's board of education.[4] Financially speaking, Will's family wasn't rich—his parents made a decent living at a time when the average income of families was only $5,600 a year, but with six people to feed and clothe and four children who needed a good education, the Smith family wasn't rolling in dough.

However, they weren't considered poor either. Will's hard-working and frugal parents were able to afford to give him a private education at Our Lady of Lourdes elementary school in Philadelphia. Our Lady of Lourdes was founded in 1908 and is staffed by the Sisters of Our Lady of Mercy, Mercedarian Friars, and teachers. Lourdes calls itself a *community* Catholic school, and its primary goal is to offer affordable, quality education to the children living in the Overbrook and Wynnefield communities.

Will worked hard at his grades at Lourdes—something his parents demanded at all times—and he was good at both science and math. But Will was also a cutup, a jokester—the kid who could easily make his family laugh while cracking jokes at dinnertime with the rest of the Smith clan. The Smith family expanded in 1971 when Will became a big brother to twin siblings Ellen and Harry.

Will had a typical childhood—he went to school, played with his friends and family, did his homework, and listened to his parents. Years later, Will would attribute his serious work ethic to his dad. He has said that his dad would work hard, laying on floors fixing refrigerators, and wanted Will to know hard work, too. So his dad tore down a brick wall in front of his store and told 12-year-old Will and his younger brother to rebuild it. Although most kids would be daunted by such a task, Will explained that he and his brother just put their heads down and laid the first brick. A year and a half later, they completed the job.

"And he said, 'Now, don't you ever tell me there's somethin' that you can't do.' And walked right through that door, went inside. And me and my brother stood here and looked. And said, 'Daddy crazy as hell, ain't he?'" Will recalled, laughing.[5] Daddy wasn't too crazy, as Will would go through a few more harsh experiences over the next few years and thanks to those lessons would know how to successfully start over and rebuild. Will finally learned the meaning of the words *work ethic*.

In the 1980s, Wynnefield's demographics changed, and more African American and middle-class residents moved into the area. When describing the religious makeup of his neighborhood, Will has said, it was "probably 50 percent Orthodox Jewish. One neighborhood over were all the pretty little Muslim girls. Mine was a Baptist household, and I went to a Catholic school. I was surrounded by different religions."[6] But during the 1980s, Wynnefield experienced a rough transformation. Gangs, drugs, and violent crime infiltrated the community.

Thirteen-year-old Will was growing up. He was now a tall, gangly teenager. At six feet two, he could easily draw attention to himself and pass as an older teen, which could have led him into an older, faster crowd. He was also at the age when curious teenagers are often drawn into experimentation and rebellious behavior. It's also a time when peer pressure—the influence of others to change an attitude, belief, or behavior—is a big problem. With the presence of gangs, drugs, and violent crime in the area, Will could easily have fallen into the negative behaviors that were running rampant in his hometown.

At the same time that Will's hometown was changing, so was his home life. As much as his parents loved Will and his siblings, their marriage was beginning to fall apart. Although Will has never spoken publicly about the reasons for the divorce, he described his parents' relationship as filled with petty arguments. He also explained that they weren't a couple that was very touchy-feely. Will Sr. and Caroline separated when Will was only 13 years old, but Will has said that unlike other divorced families, his parents' rocky relationship really didn't affect the kids in a negative way. His parents never failed to show the kids how much they were loved.

The good news was that even though his parents divorced, they were still a very strong influence in his life. It was their commitment as parents that kept Will focused on the right path. As a former member of the U.S. Air Force, Will's dad knew all about dedication, determination, hard work, and discipline, and he brought these values into his parenting. Will once said, "My father's job was to beat me into shipshape."[7] His dad was "tough but not tyrannical," according to Will. "He kept me in line. He'd get this look that said, 'One more step, Will, and it'll get ugly.'"[8]

It was this fear of his father that stopped Will from falling prey to the local drug scene: "I felt my father would kill me. Literally."[9] Stories have been told about how Will's dad would drive him to the toughest neighborhood in Philly and point out what it was like for people on drugs.

Will also considered his entire family a terrific support system, especially his older sister, Pamela: "She was an athlete—All-City track—a real overachiever. One time some guys stole money from me and I came home crying. My older sister grabbed a bat and we walked around the neighborhood looking for these guys. I remember thinking, 'Damn! This is the person you want in your corner.' My older sister always made me feel safe."[10]

When it came to his education, Will's mother Caroline said her job was to make sure that he had a strong education and a sense of respect. "Education was my goal," she said. "You learn it, you get it in your head and nobody can take it out. This was my function." She also taught him how to respect women. Will once described his mother as someone who wouldn't get into the car until he got out and opened the door for her. "Finally I'd get it—jump out, run around, open the door, apologizing: 'My fault, Mom, my fault,'" recalled Will.[11]

Will was also close to his grandmother. The Smith family lived with Will's grandmother and great-grandmother until he was about 3 years old, and even after moving out, Will remained close to them. He also said that his grandmother taught him how to treat women and to understand that God is going to make everything okay. (Will would thank her publicly later at the 2005 *American Music Awards* for teaching him to be the clean-cut man he turned out to be.) She also made certain that Will grew up as a respectful young man, a trait that would be put to the test once Will uncovered his love of rap music.

Music was always a big part of Will's childhood—he took regular piano lessons and the family participated in jam sessions—but it was in the late 1970s and 1980s when rap music came on the scene and firmly caught hold of Will's attention.

HISTORY OF RAP MUSIC

Rap music emphasizes spoken rhymes over heavy beats, and Will and his friends would often hang out in his basement and listen to this new style of music, which is also called hip-hop music. Rap started in the Bronx, New York, mostly among African Americans, Hispanics, and Latinos in the 1970s. The music used synthesizer machines and drum bands. Although many people have taken credit for starting rap music, Kool Herc is the person who seems to have started it all. He would 'call out' to the party crowds—often in basements—and then pump up the music and repeat throughout the night.

As time went on, DJs (short for disc jockeys) began to add rhymes to their call-outs and would use synthesizers to change the beat of the music. Break dancing also became popular during this time. Rapping became a street art, called *battle style*, the challenge being who could put down the other rapper the best in schoolyards and on street corners.

Popular rap artists in the 1970s included Afrika Bambaataa, who was a young gang member turned DJ (A DJ is a person who plays music for a living at parties or weddings or on the radio. Current music mogul Russell Simmons started his career in the 1970s and also convinced Kool DJ Kurt to start rapping and change his name to Kurtis Blow, an infamous name on the rap circuit. Also getting their start in the 1970s was the Sugarhill Gang. The members, all originally from New Jersey, were Wonder Mike, Big Bank Hank, and Master Gee. The group burst onto the scene with the 1979 megahit "Rapper's Delight."

Will loved "Rapper's Delight," which debuted in 1979 and instantly became a worldwide sensation. The popular 15-minute-long rap had fun, catchy lyrics, but despite its commercial success, some industry experts and artists debated whether it could really be considered one of the first rap songs. Some people suggested that the song's beat and lyrics made it a rap song, while opponents argued that true rap is supposed to be hard-core, raw, and edgy, which "Rapper's Delight" definitely wasn't.

While "Rapper's Delight" had some questionable sexual references, it was free of profanity—which was more common in harder rap music. However, Sugarhill's fans didn't seem to care about the debate, and neither did Will. The song's popularity was obvious and the Sugarhill Gang went onto sell more than eight million records worldwide.

Will loved rap music, but it was already starting to change. In the 1980s, a new form of rap—called *gangsta rap*—emerged onto the scene. The songs were filled with violent lyrics that revolved around such themes as guns, shootings, killings, drugs, and sex. When asked about the violent lyrics, gangsta rappers would say that the songs reflected the struggles of youths living in the inner city.

In the 1980s, more rappers came on the scene, including LLCool J and Tracy Marrow (otherwise known as "Ice T") who was considered a pioneer in gangsta music. Dr. Dre was part of a rap group called World Class Wreckin' Crew before he teamed up with fellow rapper Ice Cube. Grandmaster Flash and the Furious Five was highly influential in the industry and became the first rap group to ever be inducted into the Rock and Roll Hall of Fame. Other rap superstars in the 1980s were Notorious B.I.G., Run D.M.C., Snoop Dogg, Tupac Shakur, and Marion "Suge" Knight. The movement was unstoppable.

"Rap was a burgeoning movement in the '80s," explains Tracey Ford, editor of TheBoomBox.com. "Groups like The Sugarhill Gang, and Grandmaster Flash and the Furious Five introduced this movement to the masses with songs like 'Rapper's Delight' and 'The Message.' The genre was already popular in New York, the birthplace of rap and hip-hop, but the rest of the world became acquainted with it because of 'Rapper's Delight,' and [this song] was a great first impression because it combines the best aspects of the music. It showcased the importance of the DJ; properly displays the importance of having flow, and it was perfect for breakers."

WILL'S EARLY ASPIRATIONS

Will loved rap music and started having his own aspirations of one day becoming a rap superstar. So he started trying to write his own rap songs.

At first, he followed what the successful artists were doing and started writing lyrics that were filled with profanity and focused on provocative themes. However, it was Will's grandmother who read his lyrics and strongly suggested that he clean up his act and remove the profanity.

"I'll never forget what my grandmother said when she read them: 'He who is truly articulate shuns profanity,'" Will told *Essence* magazine. She convinced Will that it was a way to stand out from the other gangsta rappers. Although Will could have chosen to defy his grandmother and stick with what he wanted to do, he had been raised to show respect for his parents and grandparents. He was eager for their approval, so he honored his grandmother's request and removed the questionable lyrics. Will then performed—rapping and dancing—for anyone who would watch and listen at birthday parties and other family functions.

In 1985, Will met Jeffrey Townes, someone who would soon become an important part of his life. Townes, who nicknamed himself "DJ Jazzy (Jazz) Jeff," was born January 22, 1965, and had already been a working DJ for quite some time. Like Will, Jazz was also born in West Philadelphia and came from a very musical household. Jazz developed a love and appreciation of music at an early age and knew that he wanted to pursue it as a career. While other boys were busy playing football or baseball with friends, 10-year-old Jazz started his DJ career spinning records at parties and using his family's basement as a training ground for his expert mixing.

While Will was home, working on schoolwork by day and songwriting by night, Jazz was a student at John Bartram High in Philadelphia and already experienced at deejaying parties. He became well-known for what was known as a *scratching*, a technique a DJ uses to produce a special sound. It was made by turning the vinyl record back and forth on the turntable, creating a scratching sound.[12]

Will met Jazz when Jazz was deejaying at a friend's party. Jazz needed someone to fill in for an MC who didn't show. Will, seizing the opportunity to perform in front of an audience, stepped in. The musical chemistry between the two was palpable, and the duo became an instant hit. After the party was over, Jazz and Will decided to team up. With Will's talent for writing great song lyrics and Jazz's natural ability to scratch and spin, they did what many kids their age often do—formed a musical act in hopes of making it big one day. They also partnered with Clarence Holmes, a mutual friend in Philly, who was known for his beatboxing skills. A beatboxer is someone who produces percussion sounds with his mouth. Known as "Ready Rock C," Clarence credited Will with having a "gift with words."[13]

In the meantime, Will's interest in music and performing was growing, but he still listened to his parents and worked hard in school and achieved decent grades. After all, becoming a success in the music business was a one in a million shot, and his parents knew an education was important. Will was a consistent B student, although he once described himself as a "classic underachiever who found it hard to read an entire book."[14]

He was a student at Overbrook High School in the Overbrook section of Philadelphia. Overbrook is a four-year secondary school, and, according to 2005 statistics, 99 percent of the student population is African American. It was during his time at Overbrook High that Will earned the nickname "Prince." Many stories have been circulated about why he was given this name, but Will was the school's class clown and could talk his way out of any situation that he got himself into, so his teachers nicknamed him "Prince" (as in Prince Charming). Will later added the word *fresh* in front of Prince—*fresh* was a popular slang term at the time that meant "cool,"—and he has since been known as the "Fresh Prince."

It was the summer of 1986, and when Will wasn't studying, he was writing and recording music. Will and Jazz cowrote their first song, "Girl's Ain't Nothin but Trouble." The song, which opens with the theme from the television sitcom *I Dream of Jeannie*, focuses on a teen boy's angst about meeting girls. Ultimately, the lyrics urge boys to stay away from girls who cause nothing but trouble.

The trio worked hard to play gigs and to get their music heard. Later that year, they performed at the New Music Seminar, an annual showcase held in New York City. At this showcase, hundreds of bands and other musical acts perform for music industry insiders and hope that they can draw attention to their talents. Jazz entered the DJ competition and took first place. Winning the competition made industry execs take notice of Jazz, and it ultimately landed all three their first record deal.

On July 26, 1986, DJ Jazzy Jeff and the Fresh Prince signed a record contract with Word-Up Records Enterprises Inc. Will and Jazz had approached CEO Dana Goodman a few years earlier about signing a contract and releasing an album, but they were turned down. Later, they tried their luck again, and Goodman signed the young artists and gave them an opportunity to release a single. It was their one shot to see how the world would respond to their sound. Their debut single "Girls Ain't Nothing but Trouble" was released in 1986 on the small Word-Up label, reaching number 81 on the Rhythm & Blues (R&B) charts.

The 1980s also saw one more major change on the music scene—the advent of MTV, a cable television station launched in 1981 that played music videos all day long. It was a popular format for promoting music. DJ Jazzy Jeff and the Fresh Prince saw the potential, so they created an accompanying music video for "Girls Ain't Nothin' but Trouble."

The video tells the story of two girls that Will meets who both land him in hot water. The first girl, after finding out that Will likes her "kinda," eagerly starts pawing at him. Will responds by pushing the girl away only to have her cry foul and accuse him of assault. The second girl has Will in a compromising position when her boyfriend barges in, forcing Will to hop out the window in his shorts in the freezing cold. He suggests to the boys listening that they avoid the girls and get away when they can. The song and the video were funny, the lyrics were easy to understand, the music was catchy, and, overall, the song was one that teens could easily identify with.

For any kind of writer (songwriter, novelist, poet, etc.), the rule of thumb is to write about what you know, and perhaps "Girl's Ain't Nothin' but Trouble" could have been taken from Will's real-life girl troubles. At 16 years old, Will was into music, but like many teenage boys, he was also into girls. Will has said that talking to girls and asking them out on dates wasn't the easiest thing for him to do. He had lots of trouble getting girls to notice him, so he would often send one of his sisters or friends over to talk to the girl he was interested in. Once he knew for sure that the girl liked him, he would then make his move.[15] Unfortunately, that didn't protect young Will from getting hurt. One relationship, in particular, ended badly when the girl cheated on Will and left him heartbroken.

"I was so devastated that she cheated on me and I remember making a decision that she cheated on me cause I wasn't good enough," said Will. "And I remember laying in my mother's bed crying and making a decision that if I was the best at everything, that my woman could never cheat on me," he said. "I never wanted to be not good enough again."[16]

NEVER BEING "NOT GOOD ENOUGH AGAIN"

If the hard work and determination of Will's parents wasn't what he tapped into when pushing forward in his career, perhaps it was the heartbreak from his ex-girlfriend. Will was determined that he would never be "not good enough again." It didn't take long before he was ready to prove to the music industry and to the world that he had talent.

Although the Will and Jazz did really well on their first song, not all roads to success in the music industry are well paved. They hit a major bump in the road with their partnership with Holmes. Holmes left the group in 1990, citing creative differences, but in 1999, he filed a lawsuit against Will and Jazz, alleging that the duo owed him money from their recording profits. Holmes alleged that Will promised him, in an oral contract, a one-third share of the group's income. Holmes also claimed that Will said he would be an equal member of the group. Will denied that he owed Holmes any money and that he had created this oral contract.

Although it has been reported that Will ran into Holmes a few years later and gave him some money to help with his financial difficulties, Will claimed that those payments were only gifts to help Holmes out in a time of need. The Philadelphia District Court agreed with Will, and since it took Holmes nine years to file a lawsuit, the court denied his case, stating that the statute of limitations (the amount of time legally provided to file a court case after something occurs) had run out.

Will and Jazz would hit another bump in the road when their record label, Word-Up, sued the duo for copyright issues and the partnership ended (there is no evidence of what those copyright issues were). The pair were on their own again, but not for long. Thanks to their first single's success, DJ Jazzy Jeff and the Fresh Prince were already considered a commercial success, and other record labels took interest. It was Jive Records, a record label that had previously signed such popular 80s musical acts as Billy Ocean, Flock of Seagulls, and various hip-hop artists (they would later become known for signing pop sensations 'N Sync, the Backstreet Boys, and Britney Spears) that signed the boys. Will and Jazz released their first album, *Rock the House*, which was first released on Word-Up in 1986 but debuted on Jive in March of 1987. The album sold more than half a million copies.

Will's career as a rap star was growing, but at home he was a still a teenager who was expected to do homework. His parents were adamant that he concentrate on his education, and they expected him to go to college. At this point, Will was a senior in high school, but he switched schools, enrolling in the Julia Reynolds Masterman Laboratory and Demonstration School, a secondary school also located in Philadelphia.

The school was established in September 1958 and named for Julia Reynolds Masterman, who was instrumental in establishing the Philadelphia Home and School Council and served as its first president. It is considered one of the best college-prep public schools in Philadelphia and has been awarded several awards, including being ranked 53rd in the nation by *U.S. News and World Report* in 2007.

Academically, Will had what it took to make it into college. His grades were good enough, and he scored high on his college entrance scholastic aptitude test (SAT). The science lover that he was, he was even recommended for a scholarship to the Massachusetts Institute of Technology in Boston, Massachusetts. Will once mentioned to his mom that he wanted to be an engineer, so his practical mother had no intention of letting that dream slip away. She encouraged Will's music career wholeheartedly but suggested that he wait until he finished his college education to make all the music he wanted to. His parents didn't want their son to give up a college education to pursue a one-in-a-million shot of success in rap music.

Just because Will had a hit song and one successful rap album didn't mean that he would be able to repeat that success. Will knew, however, that this was what he wanted to do. After watching how hard his father worked to be a success and listening to his mother's arguments about the rap industry, he knew he was going to have to work even harder to prove to them he could make it.

Will and Jazz were sent off to London by their production company to record their next album. Will took this opportunity to let his parents know he had no plans of going to college when he got back to the

United States. It took some convincing since Will's mom was still making arrangements to have him attend college. Will showed them the recording contract and reminded them of the success of his hit single. He had great leverage—he already had a hit record on the radio one month before his high school graduation. It was time for Will to see where this dream was going to go, and that was enough evidence to convince his parents. He put college on the back burner and was going to continue rapping.

NOTES

1. "Ali, Will Smith and Michael Mann Q&A." *Commodore Cinema*. http://www.commodorecinema.co.uk/films/ali/more_info/qanda.html.

2. Grant, Meg. "Will Smith Interview: Will Power." *Reader's Digest.com*. Accessed August 30, 2009. http://www.rd.com/your-america-inspiring-people-and-stories/will--interview/article31133.html.

3. Doeden, Matt. *Will Smith* (*Just the Facts Biographies*). Minneapolis: Lerner Publications, 2006, p. 6. Print.

4. Grant, Meg. "Will Smith Interview: Will Power." *Reader's Digest.com*. Accessed August 30, 2009. http://www.rd.com/your-america-inspiring-people-and-stories/will--interview/article31133-3.html.

5. Kroft, Steve. "Will Smith: My Work Ethic Is 'Sickening'." *60 Minutes*. June 29, 2008. Accessed August 30, 2009. http://www.cbsnews.com/stories/2007/11/30/60minutes/main3558937.shtml.

6. Grant, Meg. "Will Power." *Reader's Digest*, December 2006.

7. "Will Smith: Love, Paranoia & the Politics of Booty." *Rolling Stone*. Accessed August 30, 2009. http://www.rollingstone.com/artists/willsmith/articles/story/5938077/cover_story_will_smith_love_paranoia__the_politics_of_booty.

8. "Will Smith's Life (the multifunctional)." *Knol: a unit of knowledge*. Accessed August 30, 2009. http://knol.google.com/k/learn-for-freedom/will-smiths-life-the-multifunctional/2ska3lxcp03tn/5#.

9. "Will Smith: Love, Paranoia & the Politics of Booty." *Rolling Stone*. Accessed August 30, 2009. http://www.rollingstone.com/artists/willsmith/articles/story/5938077/cover_story_will_smith_love_paranoia__the_politics_of_booty.

10. "Will Smith: Love, Paranoia & the Politics of Booty." *Rolling Stone*. Accessed August 30, 2009. http://www.rollingstone.com/artists/willsmith/articles/

story/5938077/cover_story_will_smith_love_paranoia__the_politics_of_booty.

11. "Will Smith: Love, Paranoia & the Politics of Booty." *Rolling Stone*. Accessed August 30, 2009. http://www.rollingstone.com/artists/willsmith/articles/story/5938077/cover_story_will_smith_love_paranoia__the_politics_of_booty.

12. DJ Jazzy Jeff. "About." http://www.djjazzyjeff.com/about/biography.

13. "Will Smith—True Hollywood Story." YouTube Video. Accessed August 30, 2009. http://www.youtube.com/watch?v=O1M3T-t14C8&feature=PlayList&p=1DE46B79CEA6F8C0&playnext=1&playnext_from=PL&index=2.

14. "Will Smith: Love, Paranoia & the Politics of Booty." *Rolling Stone*. Accessed August 30, 2009. http://www.rollingstone.com/news/story/5938077/cover_story_will_smith_love_paranoia__the_politics_of_booty/print.

15. "'Hitch' a Switch for Will Smith." *FoxNews.com*. February 11, 2005. Accessed August 30, 2009. http://www.foxnews.com/story/0,2933,147169,00.html

16. "Will Smith defends Tom Cruise, Scientology." *Access Hollywood*. Accessed August 30, 2009. http://www.msnbc.msn.com/id/22088489/.

Chapter 2

GETTIN' JIGGY WIT IT

Everything you do in your life is a move. You wake up in the morning, you strap on a gun, and you walk out on the street—that's a move. You've made a move and the universe is going to respond with its move.

—*Will Smith*

Having any kind of music career takes a lot of hard work, and the odds of making it to the top are slim. Having one hit record doesn't make an artist a success story. However, DJ Jazzy Jeff and the Fresh Prince seemed to have something different from the other rap groups. Their music was fun and clean, and thanks to that, they were exposing rap music to an audience that never would have listened to rap before—mainstream America.

If their first album, *Rock the House,* introduced DJ Jazzy Jeff and the Fresh Prince to the world, their second album, *He's the DJ, I'm the Rapper,* put them forever on the musical map (Holmes is still listed with a writer credit on the album). Released in 1988, *He's the DJ, I'm the Rapper* was rap music's first double-vinyl LP release, and it included a bonus scratch album. The album was an instant hit, and the duo immediately became multiplatinum stars. A platinum album is one that has sold more than one million units, so having a multiplatinum album means the artist has had more than one album that sold more than one million units.

Catapulting them into musical superstardom was one song in particular, "Parents Just Don't Understand." This was another fun song with lyrics to which most teens could relate. The lyrics told the story of parents who took Will shopping and chose plaid clothes and other uncool outfits for him. Will explained that parents just don't understand what kids want.

The duo received accolades from music critics for their songs and lyrics. Peter Watrous of the *New York Times* wrote, "DJ Jazzy Jeff and the Fresh Prince appeals to younger kids; the group is solidly middle class, with references to Burger King and McDonald's; the group unquestioningly embraces the American dream." Watrous said, "*Parents Just Don't Understand* is its best tune. If this doesn't have universal teen appeal, nothing does."[1]

It was the second disk that caught Watrous's attention, though, since it featured more of DJ Jazzy Jeff's turntable scratching skills: "He's a master of improvised scratching, where turntables are used percussively, and cutting, where different segments of records are mixed together in a collage. Fresh Prince joins in occasionally, but mostly it is Jazzy Jeff's accurate, unerring scratching, along with the great dance beats, that carry the album. It's hard to imagine a pop double album devoting a whole disk to instrumental tunes, especially when they feature real improvisations. It's even harder to imagine an album like that being successful."[2]

This is the album that, according to *All Music Guide to Hip-Hop: The Definitive Guide to Rap and Hip-Hop*, allowed Jeff and Will to hit commercial pay dirt. Some experts, such as *All Music Guide*, said that Will's storytelling "rhymes and antics can become hokey," but "are always good natured and fun."[3] In many ways, Jazzy Jeff and Will Smith were the perfect ambassadors for the genre. Aside from being funny, charming, and disarmingly nonthreatening, they exemplified portions of the art form that made it almost subconsciously appealing.[4]

"Parents Just Don't Understand" became the first hip-hop /rap song to ever receive a Grammy Award, an award presented annually by the National Academy of Recording Arts and Sciences of the United States for outstanding achievements in the music industry. Jazzy Jeff and Will also made a funny, colorful music video for this song, just as they had done with "Girls Ain't Nothin' but Trouble." The video won them an MTV Music Award for Best Rap Video.

The album had a few other popular singles, including the song "Brand New Funk," which was Jeff and Will's tribute to the street version of rap. It was a little edgier, compared to their last songs, although it still didn't include any questionable lyrics. The music video for "Brand New Funk" featured Will impersonating Muhammad Ali at the beginning saying, "We're gonna do this. The way it's supposed to be done. The way it's never been done before."

Another single, "Nightmare on My Street," was a parody of horror movie villain Freddy Krueger, although the song was not associated with the *Nightmare on Elm Street* franchise.

On February 1, 1995, *He's the DJ, I'm the Rapper* was certified by the Recording Industry Association of America (RIAA), a trade group that represents the music industry, as three-times platinum.

BACKLASH

Although both albums were considered a commercial success, not everybody liked Jeff and Will's idea of rap music. On the one hand, Jeff and Will's rap music was criticized by hip-hop purists who felt that the two weren't maintaining rap's rawness. Gangsta rappers would often say that their own songs were a reflection of their personal inner-city struggles. Defending his music against the gangsta rap music, Will once explained that he didn't have the same struggles as the hard-core gangsta rappers did, so instead he wrote lyrics that he as a middle-class African American could identify with—for example, kids who feel that parents don't listen to them and teenage girl problems. When asked about the backlash, Smith replied, "We make rap universal. It's more than the black experience."[5]

Tracy Ford, editor of TheBoomBox.com, explained that Will and Jeff were successful at being commercial at the beginning of their career because it was a unique way of getting their music out to the public: "The controversy is debatable, because if they didn't do things like include the *I Dream of Jeanie* theme song in their rap, would they have been able to get his music out there?"[6] Ford also said that Will wasn't attempting to compete with other rappers. He had his own sound, which allowed him and Jeff to stand out.

Ford said that Will's songs were built around teenage angst: "People who understand it and listen to it also understand frustration and they were entertained with Will. He was able to have a career without degrading women. Everybody has a start and that's where Will started. It's very impressive."[7]

Whether listeners liked the music or didn't, there was no debating the fact that the young rappers were becoming a huge mainstream success. Even though they were experiencing backlash within their own rap community, they were also enjoying the awards, accolades, fame and fortune, the likes of which two middle-class youths from Philly had never seen before. Their albums were making them millionaires, and the sales provided a nice stream of income. Will had earned a few million dollars before his 20th birthday, only a few years after starting in the business. It was a dream come true.

But remember that although Will was making millions and was a hard-working songwriter, he was still only 20 years old and didn't have a lot of experience handling his own money. Will's hard-working parents always encouraged him to save his money for his future because they knew what it was like to scrimp and save and wanted to make sure Will protected himself financially. Unfortunately, Will had other plans. These were the same plans that many people who come into a lot of money all at one time—celebrities and lottery winners, for example—have. He wanted to have a good time, so he went shopping and purchased designer clothes, cars, houses, and jewelry. Soon, Will's spending habits spiraled out of control.

While Will was enjoying the rewards of his hard work, and Hollywood was starting to take notice of his great screen presence and sense of humor in his music videos. Industry executives were anxious to see if Will could translate those music video talents into a spot on network television. Half-hour sitcoms were very popular in the 1980s and 1990s, and there were several shows that centered on an African American family or theme. *The Cosby Show,* a sitcom created by comedian Bill Cosby, was about an affluent black family and their five children. The show's spin-off, *A Different World,* centered on the life of students at a historically black college. In 1990 Will was invited to audition for roles on both

The Cosby Show and *A Different World,* but he described himself in *Jet* magazine as being "too scared" to keep the appointments.[8]

Will didn't consider himself ready for prime time just yet. However, at the same time that he was experiencing success in the music industry, musical producer Benny Medina was shopping around an idea for a brand-new television sitcom. Medina started his career with the musical group Apollo, but at 24 years old, he became the head of A&R (Artists and Repertoire—it's the division responsible for talent scouting and artist development) for Motown and worked with the legendary Berry Gordy, the founder of Motown Records.

Medina then moved onto Warner Bros. Records and became a producer, talent manager, and record executive. He has been involved in the careers of a variety of recording artists and performers, including Sean "Diddy" Combs and actress and singer Jennifer Lopez, but in the 1980s, he realized that his personal life story was worth telling. However, instead of writing an autobiography, Medina came up with the idea of a television show that would be based on his own personal experiences. Medina grew up poor and was shuffled from foster home to foster home and into youth detention centers. Medina was fortunate because, later on, he was taken in by a wealthy white family in Beverly Hills.

Medina ran into Will at a taping of *The Arsenio Hall Show* and suggested that the rapper give him a call to talk about the idea. In the meantime, Medina took his idea to music producer Quincy Jones, whom he knew because of other projects they had worked on together. "I felt that Quincy was going to have a lot of sensitivity to the project," said Medina.[9]

In his autobiography, Jones, who hadn't produced or created any television shows up until that point, explained how he felt when he read the script: "I was attracted to the idea for the show after talking with Benny Medina, whose life formed the core of the story. Jack Elliot, who used to conduct for Jacqueline Francois when I worked for the Barclays in Paris, had taken parentless Benny out of the ghetto and installed him in an apartment over the garage of his Beverly Hills home, which was shared with his son Alan."[10]

"Later, along with the executive producers Andy and Susan Borowitz, the decision was made to shift the situation so that the hosts were black bourgeois relatives, which makes it even more interesting in terms of the clash of culture and gives it more of a fish-out-of-water humor," said Jones. "The black experience is a funny experience," he said. "It's very rich. It's colorful. It's the juice of American pop culture."[11]

Quincy Jones, who ultimately sold Medina's show concept to NBC, knew the show could be a winning series if it was built around a character portrayed by Will Smith, who was becoming extremely popular. However, Will once said that nobody ever asked if he could act.

The top brass at NBC were thinking the same thing, and they needed more convincing that Will could hold a show before signing the Fresh Prince to an acting contract. After all, lead acting roles were never given to anyone who didn't have some sort of acting background. Although Will had performed in his music videos, being the star of a weekly half-hour sitcom was worlds apart from filming a music video.

To help convince the powers that be that Will had what it took to be the star of the show, Jones invited Will and the head honchos of NBC to his house so they could meet the rapper and see him in action. "Will came into Los Angeles to Quincy Jones' house, sat on the couch and said, 'Yeah, I could do this,'" said Warren Littlefield, former NBC president. "He just read a scene and it was magic." Five minutes later, Will got the job, but it didn't come without other challenges.[12]

For example, Jones also had to assure the network's sponsors that rappers such as Will weren't dangerous, a common reputation they had to overcome. "Imagine Will Smith and Jazzy Jeff being dangerous! Please!" said Jones. "Will is one of the smartest and most centered young people I've met. The first day of shooting, Will didn't know where the camera was—but he learned fast, and grew like a weed."[13] After the show went on the air, Jones went on to write the opening music for the sitcom as well as the music for in-between scenes.

Another challenge was teaching Will how to act in front of a camera. The first day of Will's television acting career was also the first day that *The Fresh Prince of Bel-Air* was taping. But what Will lacked in acting experience, he made up for in charisma and humor. However, compared to rapping in front of a camera, which seemed to come naturally to Will, acting in the television format was quite a challenge for him. "I was a nervous wreck," he recalled. "I was trying so hard. I would memorize the entire script, then I'd be lipping everybody's lines while they were talking. When I watch those [early] episodes it's disgusting. My performances were horrible."[14]

Another behind-the-scenes challenge getting *The Fresh Prince of Bel-Air* from paper to screen was getting approval for the pilot script. "When we handed in the first draft of the script, the network freaked out," said Susan Borowitz, a veteran of *Family Ties* who wrote *The Fresh Prince* pilot episode with her husband, Andy, and was also a coproducer. "They were expecting 'Crocodile Dundee' and 'Beverly Hills Cop' and were quite taken aback by the Malcolm X poster' that Mr. Smith's character hangs in his bedroom."[15]

CAST OF CHARACTERS

A successful television show consists of more than just a good script. It also requires a solid supporting cast, and the producers worked hard to put together a talented bunch of actors to work with Will. Will portrayed Will Smith, who moved from Philadelphia to Bel-Air, California, to stay with his Uncle Phil and Aunt Vivian. Philip Banks, otherwise known as "Uncle Phil," was played by veteran actor James Avery. Avery once said that he resisted Hollywood for fear that his size—six feet four, and 250 pounds—would typecast him. "I didn't want to be the big, dumb black guy on the corner," he explains.[16]

Although Uncle Phil came across as a money-tight Republican, he was also once an activist for the civil rights movement and actually heard Malcolm X speak, something that later impressed Will. Philip was an attorney who attended Princeton University and Harvard Law School. He was a member of the NAACP and became a judge later in the series. Uncle Phil was hard on Will, but he treated him like he was his own son. Ironically, Avery's size ended up being the butt of jokes between his character and Will.

When reading for the part, Avery had no idea who Will Smith was in real-life and had never heard any of his music. He only knew that he was reading for the part with a rapper. When Avery entered the room, Will was sitting at the end of the table with his feet on the edge and his hat turned sideways. Avery remembers telling Will to put his feet down, turn his hat around, and look at him when he was spoken to. Will respected the veteran actor and did as he requested, and Avery was given the part of Uncle Phil.

Vivian Banks, known as "Aunt Viv" to Will, was a professor of black history at the University of California, Los Angeles (UCLA). Vivian was played by Janet Hubert-Whitten in seasons one, two, and three and by Daphne Maxwell Reid in seasons four through six. Hubert-Whitten had landed just a few acting roles before she earned the role on *The Fresh Prince*. Hilary Banks, Will's oldest cousin, was played by Karyn Parsons. Before earning this role, Parsons had other minor acting roles when she landed the role of the attractive, but spoiled and unintelligent Hilary.

Alfonso Ribeiro played Carlton Banks, Will's nerdy, preppy, and conservative cousin—and standard sitcom sidekick—who really did care about Will, although they both argued and bantered with insulting jokes. Ribeiro had been acting and dancing since he was eight years old, appeared on Broadway in *The Tap Dance Kid*, and starred in another popular television sitcom, *Silver Spoons*, before becoming his most well-known and most popular character, Carlton. Ribeiro created a signature wacky, wacky dance routine for Carlton that he broke into when his favorite crooner Tom Jones was playing on the stereo. The writers also used Carlton's virginity as a running gag in the show, until he lost it several seasons later.

The young Tatyana M. Ali was very familiar with Will Smith and his rap music way before she earned the part of Ashley Banks. She once said that Will's music was the only rap music that her parents allowed her to listen to as a child. Ali started her career at the tender age of seven, performing on *Sesame Street* and winning the television talent show *Star Search* twice. Her character Ashley was the youngest of Will's three cousins and looked up to Will. She was a smart girl, who also wanted to be independent and out from under the thumb of her overprotective father. On several occasions, Ashley started acting out, and her father would often blame Will and the Philadelphia culture to which he exposed Ashley.

Joseph Marcell was an English actor who had some minor television roles before landing the role of Geoffrey Barbara Butler, the Banks family's cynical butler who eventually developed a very close relationship with Will. Even Will's real-life musical partner, DJ Jazzy Jeff, made regular appearances in the show as Will's annoying, unintelligent best friend who came from the lower-income Compton, California, area. This was Jeff's first foray into acting as well, other than recording the music videos. On the show, Jeff's character became smitten with Hilary, but Hilary didn't feel the same way about him. Jeff eventually marries and divorces. Jeff also had an often-repeated gag on the show—when Uncle Phil got annoyed with him, the audience got to watch Uncle Phil throw Jeff out of the house.

AFRICAN AMERICANS ON TELEVISION

The Fresh Prince of Bel-Air wasn't a groundbreaking show for African Americans—although it did break ground for including rap and hip-hop music and culture themes. There had already been many network sitcoms before *The Fresh Prince* that centered on low-income as well as affluent black families. In the 1970s, *Good Times* (which ran from 1974 to 1979) centered on the day-to-day life of the Evans family, a low-income family that lived in the projects in the South Side of Chicago. The show's characters included Florida, James, and their three children—J.J., Thelma, and Michael. The show was a spin-off of the sitcom *Maude*, and it regularly stayed in the top 25 ratings spots. In the last two years of its run, its popularity began to fade, and it was canceled.

Another sitcom, *What's Happening*, featuring Raj, Dwayne, Rerun, Dee, Shirley, and Mama, centered on a lower-class black neighborhood in the Watts section of Los Angeles, California. The show ran from 1976 to 1979 to good ratings. In 1978, *Diff'rent Strokes* debuted and focused on two kids from the projects of Harlem, New York, who were adopted by Mr. Drummond, their mother's rich employer, after she died. *Diff'rent Strokes* seemed similar to Medina's life, since the kids were adopted by a white family, but not all the parallels were similar. The comedy was a hit that ran for eight years.

The Fresh Prince of Bel-Air also wasn't the first sitcom to highlight the day-to-day escapades of a wealthy black family. *The Jeffersons*, which featured the low-income next-door neighbors from the 1970s sitcom *All in the Family*, focused on the life of George Jefferson, the owner of a dry-cleaning business, his wife, son, maid, and mixed-race neighbors. As a character first on *All in the Family*, George Jefferson ended up opening five dry-cleaning stores in the New York area, which allowed him to "move on up" to a penthouse apartment and, of course, to his own show. *The Jeffersons* ran for eight years, from 1975 to 1983.

There were a few other sitcoms throughout the years that focused on African Americans, too, including *227,* which centered on a housewife and her friends and tenants in the apartment in which she lived. It ran for five years from 1985 to 1990. *Amen* focused on a deacon, played by Sherman Hemsley, who had previously played George Jefferson, and his family and church members. It debuted in 1986 and also ran for five years. Six years before the debut of *The Fresh Prince* was the debut of *The Cosby Show,* which ran from 1984 to 1992. *The Cosby Show* is considered one of the most successful and longest-running hits in American television history. The show centered on an upper-middle-class family, the Huxtables, consisting of a doctor (Cliff) and a lawyer (Claire), and their children Sondra, Theo, Denise, Vanessa, and Rudy.

WILL'S PERFORMANCE

The Fresh Prince of Bel-Air debuted on NBC's Monday night schedule in the fall of 1990. The show focused on Will's character, also named Will Smith, a teen who was sent from his troubled neighborhood in Philadelphia to live with the Banks family—made up of his aunt, uncle, and cousins, plus their butler—whose members were wealthy and had extreme Republican viewpoints. Although viewers believed the show was based on Will Smith's real life, especially since the opening number resembled the sounds of Will's real-life rap songs, it was actually based on Medina's life, with just a few minor tweaks.

Will was nervous about his performance and, of course, he had the right to be nervous. After all, he was a 21-year-old rap star with no prior acting experience taking on the lead role in a sitcom that was expected to do very well. There was also the added pressure of producing another show that centered on an African American family, but whose main character was into rap music and its culture. The show also had a cast that wasn't composed of big-name television stars at the time, so Will was the most well-known name on the show.

However, Will didn't feel that there was extra pressure on him to make the show successful. He said, "That's pressure for (the producers). If the show doesn't go well for me, I won't be any worse off. The pressure is on NBC."[17] There were high expectations for the show. *The New York Times* even called it a "programming gamble" to see if hip-hop could reach out and attract a mainstream television audience, but they agreed that it was the most highly touted show of the fall season.[18] The sitcom's other network competition included *Uncle Buck*, a sitcom based on the movie of the same name, as well as the adventure series *MacGyver* and Fox's *Night at the Movies*.

Even Karyn Parsons, who played Hilary, wasn't quite sure the show would be a hit, so she kept her part-time job as a waitress until she knew for sure. "Will, James, Benny and all the guys would come by and laugh and point at me through the window. They would bang on the window, 'What are you doing here? We have a TV show.' I'm thinking, I don't know what's going to happen with that show! You just don't know. I quit once it was picked up. It's the same thing with Will. Although you know he's incredibly charismatic, it doesn't mean that you thought, Hey, he's going to be this megastar. You aren't surprised, but when you are just hanging out with him, you aren't thinking, You are going to be King of The Universe someday."[19]

The premier episode—when Will moves in with the Banks family and causes a ruckus along the way—finished in 16th place for that week, which is considered a great start for a new show. The following week, the show dropped to 40th place behind *Uncle Buck*. It was a drop that already had industry members forecasting changes on the show, including a potential change with the writers, Andy and Susan Borowitz. The writers said they were very pleased with the ratings And the network was too. They thought the show had potential and hoped that audiences would give it a chance.

That's exactly what audiences did, and it paid off. According to the ratings and the critics, the first season didn't disappoint, and Parsons never returned to her waitress job. The sitcom was praised for its comedic writing. "The writers and cast made all of these familiar elements work because they never allowed us to take the whole affair too seriously. Rather, they loaded the show with self-deprecating humor. (Will got a haircut and the barber said, "Now you know I'm gonna have to charge you extra for cuttin' around the ears?"); breaks in the fourth wall (after making a basket, Will turned to the camera and proclaimed, "I'm going' to Disneyland!"); self referential humor (Philip commented to his wife,

"Vivian, you are so naïve. You would believe Will If he told you that he was some big rap star whose album just went platinum."); and down-right silliness (Geoffrey's last name was Butler and his middle name was Barbara.)"[20]

Every season, *The Fresh Prince of Bel-Air* writers stretched beyond comedy to also tackle tougher topics, such as racism and violence. For example, in episode six of the first season, entitled "Mistaken Identity," Carlton and Will were arrested because the cops, who were white, believed the boys had stolen the car they were driving in and were responsible for other car thefts in the area. However, they were actually driving the car from one location to another as a favor to Uncle Phil's law-firm partner. Will was convinced that the white police officers pulled them over simply because they were two young black kids, while Carlton told Will that the cops were just doing their job. As a result, Carlton's faith in fair treatment is tested. In another episode, Will was shot when he jumped in front of a robber who was attempting to shoot Carlton while robbing them at the ATM. Carlton feared for his life and bought a gun for protection. Other episodes have focused on drug use and sex.

KNOCK, KNOCK, IT'S THE IRS

While audiences were giving *The Fresh Prince of Bel-Air* a chance and everything seemed to be going well, Will had some problematic aspects of his private life to repair. He was living on his own in an apartment in Burbank, California, far from the protective eye of his parents. Will had a successful, and lucrative, recording career and was working on what was becoming a hit television show. However, privately, he had to deal with real-life grown-up problems. Will was spending way too much money. In addition, he was a bright young man, but naïve, and didn't understand how show business worked behind the scenes. As a result, the Internal Revenue Service (IRS) claimed that he didn't pay taxes on the money he had made as a rapper.

Will's spending was out of control, and he was in debt to the IRS for a whopping $2.8 million in back taxes that he owed on the small fortune he had made as a rapper. Luckily, he wasn't in serious trouble, but all of his purchases had to be returned in order to repay his debt. In addition, the

IRS took 70 percent of each paycheck that he earned on *The Fresh Prince* for the first three years. It was a lesson that Will wouldn't soon forget. "There's nothing more sobering than having six cars and a mansion one day and you can't even buy gas for the cars the next," said Will.[21]

While Will's television career was off to a good start, DJ Jazzy Jeff and the Fresh Prince struggled a little with their next album, *And in This Corner*, released in 1989. The lead single was "I Think I Can Beat Mike Tyson," and the accompanying music video included fellow sitcom costars James Avery and Alfonso Ribeiro. Although album sales were considered successful—it reached gold—new faces had emerged on the rap scene, adding more competition for listeners, and the duo's popularity was beginning to slip.

At this point, Jeff and Will made a strategic business decision to take a step back from their music career and just focus on the television show for a while. However, it's interesting how the Hollywood cycle works; since Will had a hit television show on his resume, the music of DJ Jazzy Jeff and the Fresh Prince was soon in hot demand again. The pair responded to the attention by releasing another album, *Homebase*, in 1991. This album included the megahit single "Summertime," which was about just that—sitting back and relaxing and unwinding. On this album and in the video, Will sounded and looked a bit more mature, a bit more grown-up. Another single from the album, "You Saw My Blinker," was a humorous song about an elderly lady who crashed into pop singer Prince's new car. The song reached #20 on Billboard's Hot 100 and #22 on Hot R&B/Hip-Hop singles. Overall, the album was incredibly successful, reaching platinum status and earning the duo yet another Grammy Award.

WILL AND THE LADIES

Everything was falling into place for Will. *The Fresh Prince of Bel-Air* was doing well in the ratings, Will's acting skills improved, and his music career was holding steady. Although the young, single Will was popular with the fans and the ladies, his social life was lacking a little bit, but that wouldn't last for long. In the early 1990s, a young actress, 24-year-old Sheree Elizabeth Zampino, who Will met while they were both visiting the set of *A Different World*, turned his head and stole his heart.

Sheree is an actress of Italian and African American descent and when she met Will, she was a model and fashion-design student. Will said he fell in love with her immediately, but Sheree didn't feel the same way about Will. She played hard to get, only giving Will a phone number but no date. Will tried very hard for six months to convince Sheree to go out with him until she finally agreed to go on a first date. "But I knew," Will said. "You know how you can feel it? When your charm is over-powering someone and they can't defend themselves?" he said. "And every attempt that they make to keep themselves from falling just makes them fall harder."[22]

Several months into their relationship, Will and Sheree had an un-expected surprise—Sheree was pregnant! Twenty-three-year-old Will was ready to settle down and start a family, so he surprised Sheree by pro-posing to her on Christmas Eve, 1991. Will, a self-proclaimed romantic, convinced Sheree that he had left to fly home to Philly for the holidays: "What I actually did was go to the airport to meet my brother. He'd flown in specially just to bring me a diamond ring that I'd bought from a friend back east. I got the ring and went home. Then I called Sheree, pretend-ing I was still at the airport. I told her I'd forgotten some really important papers. Could she go to my L.A. home, grab them, and bring them to me at the airport."[23] Sheree said yes, and the couple was married on May 9, 1992. On November 11, 1992, their son, William C. Smith III, was born. The couple nicknamed him "Trey," which means *three*.

NOTES

1. "Rap Enters the Album Age and the Mainstream." *The New York Times.* Accessed August 30, 2009. http://query.nytimes.com/gst/fullpage.html?res=94 0DEED91F30F931A25755C0A96E948260&pagewanted=2.

2. "Rap Enters the Album Age and the Mainstream." *The New York Times.* Accessed August 30, 2009. http://query.nytimes.com/gst/fullpage.html?res=94 0DEED91F30F931A25755C0A96E948260&pagewanted=2.

3. *All music guide to hip-hop the definitive guide to rap & hip-hop.* San Francisco, CA: Backbeat Books. Distributed to the book trade in the U.S. and Canada by Group West. Distributed to the music trade in the U.S. and Canada by Hal Leonard Pub., 2003, p. 121.

4. "The Globalization of Beats & Rhymes." *PopMatters.* Accessed Au-gust 30, 2009. http://www.popmatters.com/music/features/060620-djjazzyjeff. shtml.

5. "Will Smith." *VIBE Magazine*. Accessed August 30, 2009. http://www.vibe.com/celebs/about.html?id=50.

6. Tracy Ford, interview with author, June 24, 2009.

7. Tracy Ford, interview with author, June 24, 2009.

8. "Will Smith Biography—Grew up in a Loving Family, Entered the Music Business as a Teen." *Brief Biographies*. Accessed August 30, 2009. http://biography.jrank.org/pages/2827/Smith-Will.html.

9. Gunther, Marc. "TELEVISION: Black Producers Add a Fresh Nuance." *New York Times*. August 26, 1990. http://www.nytimes.com/1990/08/26/arts/television-black-producers-add-a-fresh-nuance.html?pagewanted=all.

10. Jones, Quincy. *Q: The Autobiography of Quincy Jones*. New York: Harlem Moon, 2002, p. 298. Print.

11. Gunther, Marc. "TELEVISION: Black Producers Add a Fresh Nuance." *New York Times*. August 26, 1990.http://www.nytimes.com/1990/08/26/arts/television-black-producers-add-a-fresh-nuance.html?sec=&spon=&pagewanted=all.

12. "Will Smith: Love, Paranoia & the Politics of Booty." *Rolling Stone*. Accessed August 30, 2009. http://www.rollingstone.com/artists/willsmith/articles/story/5938077/cover_story_will_smith_love_paranoia__the_politics_of_booty#

13. "Will Smith's Life (the multifunctional)." *Knol: a unit of knowledge*. Accessed August 30, 2009. http://knol.google.com/k/learn-for-freedom/will-smiths-life-the-multifunctional/2ska3lxcp03tn/5?domain=knol.google.com&locale=en#.

14. "Will Smith Biography—Grew up in a Loving Family, Entered the Music Business as a Teen." *Brief Biographies*. Accessed August 30, 2009. http://biography.jrank.org/pages/2827/Smith-Will.html.

15. "'Fresh Prince of Bel Air' Puts Rap in Mainstream." *The New York Times*. Accessed August 30, 2009. http://query.nytimes.com/gst/fullpage.html?res=9C0CE7D61131F934A2575AC0A966958260&sec=&spon=&pagewanted=all.

16. "James Avery's Real-Life Role: The Indomitable Pro." *San Jose Mercury News*. September 23, 1996. *NewsLibrary.com*. Accessed August 30, 2009. http://nl.newsbank.com/nl-search/we/Archives?p_product=SJ&s_site=mercurynews&p_multi=SJ&p_theme=realcities&p_action=search&p_maxdocs=200&p_topdoc=1&p_text_direct-0=0EB72006C57C4839&p_field_direct-0=document_id&p_perpage=10&p_sort=YMD_date:D&s_trackval=GooglePM.

17. "'Fresh Prince of Bel Air' Puts Rap in Mainstream." *The New York Times*. Accessed August 30, 2009. http://query.nytimes.com/gst/fullpage.html?res=9C0CE7D61131F934A2575AC0A966958260.

18. "'Fresh Prince of Bel Air' Puts Rap in Mainstream." *The New York Times*. Accessed August 30, 2009. http://query.nytimes.com/gst/fullpage.html?res=9C0CE7D61131F934A2575AC0A966958260.

19. "Karyn Parsons: The Fresh Princess." *Essence Magazine*. Accessed August 30, 2009. http://www.essence.com/news_entertainment/entertainment/articles/karynparsonsthefreshprincess.

20. Bloom, Ken, and Frank Vlastnik. *Sitcoms The 101 Greatest TV Comedies of All Time*. New York: Black Dog & Leventhal, 2007.

21. "Can Will Smith Play On Park Avenue?" *EW.com*. December 24, 1993. http://www.ew.com/ew/article/0,,309042,00.html.

22. "Will Smith & Sheree Zampino." *Wed TV*. May 9, 1992. Accessed August 30, 2009. http://www.geocities.com/wedtvsite/celeb_willsshereez.html.

23. "Will Smith & Sheree Zampino." *Wed TV*. May 9, 1992. Accessed August 30, 2009. http://www.geocities.com/wedtvsite/celeb_willsshereez.html.

Chapter 3

SOPHOMORE YEAR

The Fresh Prince of Bel-Air took a little time to grow an audience during its first season, but by its sophomore year, it had clearly settled in to become a solid ratings winner. The show was also paired with another successful Monday night NBC sitcom, *Blossom*, a half-hour sitcom that focused on a young teenage girl's life at home with her single dad. NBC cross-promoted the two shows, with Will Smith even making an appearance on *Blossom*. At this point, Will was becoming much more comfortable on camera, and the television critics began to notice. "Smith seems so spontaneous, so much at ease in front of the camera, that it's frequently hard to tell which of his lines are scripted and which are ad-libbed," said Ken Tucker, critic with *Entertainment Weekly*.[1]

Tucker also said that the ratings for *The Fresh Prince* kept going up in seasons two and three because "the series is one of the few on TV that consistently acknowledges a full range of African American lives—all social and economic classes are represented, and they eye each other with both suspicion and sympathy."[2]

Although he was still a self-proclaimed silly, goofy guy, Will was growing up and was starting to get serious about his entire career and the choices he was making. Barely into his second year of acting, Will knew that he wanted to go one step further. He wanted to be a success on the big screen as well. He already had a successful music career and was on a hit television show, but he was plotting his next career move.

While other hard-working actors, especially those who were also newlyweds and new parents, would use summer vacations to take a break from work, that wasn't Will Smith. Will wanted to use his summer vacations from television to appear in movies, especially those that allowed him to stretch his acting abilities. So when an opportunity came along to play a more serious role in *Where the Day Takes You*—and the opportunity to earn a $50,000 paycheck—Will didn't hesitate to sign on the dotted line.

The 1992 movie *Where the Day Takes You*, directed by Marc Rocco, and focuses on several teenage runaways who are trying to survive living on the streets of Los Angeles. *Where the Day Takes You* follows the homeless kids throughout Hollywood's underground as they use drugs, panhandle, and sell their bodies to earn money for food and other needs. The kids become a family, with the character King as their leader. When King is accused of murder, the rest of the kids have to figure out how to get along without him, which they don't have an easy time doing. The movie depicts their relationships with each other and with King, who acts in a parental role.

This movie gave Will an opportunity to step away from his wisecracking character on *The Fresh Prince of Bel-Air* to play a more serious role as a homeless, legless teenager. The film was critically acclaimed and nominated for the Critics Award at the Deauville Film Festival. It also won the Golden Space Needle Award at the Seattle International Film Festival. The rest of the cast included up-and-coming actors Dermot Mulroney, Sean Astin, Balthazar Getty, Lara Flynn Boyle, Ricki Lake, James LeGros, Laura San Giacomo, David Arquette, and Christian Slater.

Will's next role was as Tea Cake Walters in the 1993 movie *Made in America*, starring Whoopi Goldberg, Ted Danson, and Nia Long (Nia became Will's on-screen love interest in *The Fresh Prince of Bel-Air*). The movie is about a single black woman, played by Goldberg, who conceives a child with the help of a sperm-bank donor, played by Danson. When her daughter discovers the truth about her parentage and wants to find out who her father is, she discovers that her dad is a white car dealer. The movie grossed more than $44 million, but it took a beating from the critics. Will's part was small, but notable, and he doubled his salary from the previous movie, to $100,000.

Although Will's natural acting talent was getting him noticed, what was interesting was that he was never the type of man who believed he actually had any talent. He says, "I considered myself above slightly above average when it came to talent, but what separated me from the others was a seriously sick work ethic."[3]

A work ethic is a set of values based on the moral virtues of hard work and diligence, and Will was beginning to prove just how "seriously sick" his work ethic was. Will earned small, yet notable, movie roles, but he did everything he could with each role in order to stand out and become better. Will worked hard to convince director Fred Schepisi that he was perfect for the part of Paul in *Six Degrees of Separation*. "Everybody got excited about Will, but I was a little more cautious," admitted Schepisi. "I interviewed a lot of actors. But Will tried to convince me that he'd do whatever it would take, would go through whatever process, was sure he could get himself prepared. That confidence and charm was everything the character should be. (He was) worth taking a chance on."[4]

Will had already been turned down for other roles, including the one that was given to comedian Arsenio Hall in Eddie Murphy's *Coming to America*. His meeting with John Guare, the writer for *Six Degrees*, didn't go well at first. Guare refused to meet with Will regardless of how much studying and preparation Will had done. Finally, when Guare walked into Will's dressing room on the set of *The Fresh Prince* and saw his pictures of Malcolm X and Chairman Mao, he asked Will to explain why he had those posters. When Will started to explain, Guare interrupted, telling Will, "be quiet, you're him."[5]

That *him* would be Paul, a role that would really challenge Will's acting abilities. Paul is a gay man and a con artist who cons his way into the lives of a New York City couple (played by veteran actors Stockard Channing and Donald Sutherland) and convinces them that he is legendary actor Sidney Poitier's son and that he has been mugged. Will was thrilled that he got the role, and has said that getting this part was one of the happiest days of his life. He knew that doing well in a role like that would open doors.[6]

The role of a homosexual con artist came at a time in Will's life when he was ready to break out of his weekly sitcom character that viewers identified him with the most. Will *was The Fresh Prince of Bel-Air*, and while that was a great starting point for his career, he wanted more. The question was whether anyone else would take him seriously as a dramatic actor.

To improve his acting skills, Will trained with an acting and dialect coach, but it was veteran actor Donald Sutherland who had to teach Will about how to behave properly on the set. Sutherland is a well-respected actor who has had a film career for more than 50 years, starring in such great films as *MASH* and *The Dirty Dozen*. Will was used to being the rambunctious actor who pumped up the audiences during *The Fresh Prince of Bel-Air* warm-ups, but he had to mature and tone it down for the set of the movie. It was Sutherland—who had never even heard of Will before he got the role of Paul—who took him aside and honestly told him to shut up. Will replied, "I'm totally fine with someone who said, 'I think it's time to work now.'"[7]

Playing Paul was a great role for Will—and it earned him a cool half-million-dollar salary—but it wasn't without some controversy. Will knew that the script called for a lip-lock with costar Anthony Michael Hall, whose character has a crush on Paul. The movie came at a time period when only some straight actors were playing the limited number of gay lead characters. Until this point, some good examples of this were in the movies *Sunday Bloody Sunday*, *Dog Day Afternoon*, *Kiss of the Spider Woman*, and *Philadelphia*. In *Philadelphia*, for example, Tom Hanks plays a gay lawyer who contracts AIDS.

Today, there are more straight actors that will play a gay role than ever before—for example, the late Heath Ledger was nominated for his performance as a gay cowboy in the 2005 movie *Brokeback Mountain*. In 2008, Sean Penn won an Academy Award for his portrayal of California's first openly gay elected official, Harvey Milk, in *Milk*. But Will wasn't ready to take that step in his career. Looking back, he knows that it was the wrong decision, but at the time, he wasn't emotionally ready to make the leap. "It was very immature on my part," Smith said. "I was thinking, 'How are my friends in Philly going to think about this?' I wasn't emotionally stable enough to artistically commit to that aspect of the film."[8]

To solve the dilemma, the director used a stand-in actor for filming the actual kiss, making sure to film only the back of the actors' heads. *Six Degrees of Separation* received good reviews, although Will's reviews were mixed. The *New York Times* critic Janet Maslin reported, "The film's only casting misstep comes with Mr. Smith, who plays Paul as a smooth, pleasant interloper without the hints of mockery or desperation that should accompany his deception. Mr. Smith recites his lines plausibly without bringing great passion to the role."[9]

However, the *Movie Vault* reviewer, Megan Barnet, disagreed, as did much of Hollywood: "The plot is anchored by Will Smith's Paul. Smith is the film's 'burst of colour,' both literally, as the only black actor in the film, and metaphorically. Flanders, describing one of his Cézanne paintings, said 'A burst of colour has to carry so much.' And with the wonderful performance by Will Smith, Paul provides a common link and inspiration for the film — a 'burst of colour' in Ouisa and Flanders' sombre aristocratic world."[10]

During this extremely busy time in his life, Will could have focused on excelling at just one aspect of his career—television, movies, or music—but he chose not to give up on any of them. Instead, he figured out how to make it all work and dedicated himself to every one of his opportunities.

He teamed up with Jazz to record and release *Code Red*, the fifth album by the duo, on October 12, 1993. Unfortunately, the album wasn't as successful as Will and Jazz's previous releases, although it would be certified gold by the Recording Association of America. It included three singles—"Boom! Shake the Room," "I'm Looking for the One to Be With Me," and "I Wanna Rock"—that reached the charts, but it only peaked at 64th place on the Billboard Top 200 and 39th place on the Top R&B/Hip-Hop charts. Was the popularity of DJ Jazzy Jeff and the Fresh Prince faltering again?

Not necessarily. The music industry was changing, and Will and Jazz were facing even more competition in the rap category than they did when they released their first album. Gangsta rap had grown since it was introduced in the 1980s and had become even more popular over the last decade. Artists such as Dr. Dre and Tupac Shakur dominated the industry in the 90s, both in sales and popularity. Shakur grew up in Oakland, California, and broke into the industry with the group Digital

Underground. His music made references to cop killings and sexual violence. Like Will, Shakur was also starting to get movie roles—in *Juice* in 1992 and *Poetic Justice* in 1993. He eventually sold more than 65 million albums in the course of his short career, until his tragic death when he was gunned down several years later.

According to Dr. Dre's biography, *Dr. Dre: The Biography by Ronin Ro*, "Dre pioneered gangsta rap and his own variation of the sound, G-Funk. Boogie Down Productions' early albums were hardcore but cautionary tales of the criminal mind, but Dre's records with NWA celebrated the hedonistic, amoralistic side of gang life." Although the public still loved Will's music and Jazz's scratching, it was obvious that the tastes of rap-loving listeners were changing. "When I was doing it, rap was kind of uplifting, and now it seems to be completely ignorant and socially degenerate and misogynistic," said Will. "It's very different from the rap world that I grew up in."[11]

In the meantime, *The Fresh Prince of Bel-Air* continued to be a ratings winner, and Will earned additional executive control on the show. Behind the scenes, however, conflict started to brew. It had been reported that there was a war of words between Will's on-screen mother, Janet Hubert-Whitten, and Will. In the third season, Hubert-Whitten was pregnant in real life and said she was living in "hormone hell."[12] She admitted she snapped at crew members but blamed it on the difficult pregnancy and her 65-pound weight gain. The real-life pregnancy was written into the series, but it was said that at one point, Hubert-Whitten blamed Will for her problems on the set.

What was the truth? It depended on what tabloids you read or who you listened to at the time. On the one hand, Will was quoted as saying that Hubert-Whitten brought a lot of her problems to work and these problems lasted well beyond her pregnancy. Will allegedly told a radio station, "I can say straight up that Janet Hubert-Whitten wanted the show to be 'The Aunt Viv of Bel-Air Show,' because I know she is going to dog me in the press . . . She has basically gone from a quarter of a million dollars a year to nothing. She's mad now but she's been mad all along. She said once, 'I've been in the business for 10 years and this snotty-nosed punk comes along and gets a show.' No matter what, to her I'm just the AntiChrist."[13]

When interviewed about her side of the conflict, Hubert-Whitten said that Will had a tremendous amount of clout on the show and that he was responsible for having her appearances in the sitcom reduced from 25 to 13 episodes. She also claimed that Will had her salary cut in half as well. "They (NBC officials) kept calling me asking me to say the parting was mutual, but I'm not like that," she said. "I fight back."[14]

Hubert-Whitten didn't agree to the new contract, and while heated discussions were going back and forth, she decided to accept another contract option. That is, until the producers decided that it was too late and they let her go. Will insisted in a later interview that he told Hubert-Whitten the situation wasn't his doing, but his former costar failed to believe him. He then said, "I think that the show suffered for the loss of Janet Hubert-Whitten."[15]

Hubert-Whitten filed a lawsuit against the show and against Will, charging slander, emotional distress, and negligence, but the case was later dismissed. When Hubert-Whitten left, actress Daphne Maxwell Reid took her place at the start of season four and played Aunt Viv until the show ended. Reid had roles on such shows as *WKRP in Cincinnati*, *The Love Boat*, *The A-Team*, *Cagney & Lacey*, *Hill Street Blues*, and more before taking over as Vivian Banks.

When Reid took over the part, Nicky, the fourth Banks child, was also added to the show. Although there may have been tension behind the scenes, the show never suffered in the ratings, even after Hubert-Whitten left. *The Fresh Prince* writers even poked a little fun at having to switch mothers during the series. During one episode, Jazz remarked, "You know Mrs. Banks, there's something different about you."

The next season, baby Nicky experienced what is known as a television-magic growth spurt, growing from a newborn baby to a pre-schooler in just one season. And again, the writers took liberties with the Daphne Maxwell Reid cast change as Jazz quipped, "So who's playing the mother this season?"

This was also the season in which the writers delved more into Will's past and decided it was time to bring his dad back. Up until this point in the series, Will's dad had not appeared. It was just known that he left when Will was young. This particular episode, entitled "Papa's Got a Brand-New Excuse," which ran on May 9, 1994, was one of the most memorable episodes of the entire *Fresh Prince* series. Will's father, Lou (played by Ben Vereen), returned and made Will a promise to take him on the road with him. Will was happy to be reconnecting with his father, but once he had packed and was ready to go, Lou withdrew the offer, saying that he had a big deal he was working on and that Will just couldn't come along.

The next part of the scene was a powerful conversation between Will and Uncle Phil, in which Will angrily told Uncle Phil how well he had lived his life without his dad so far, and that what had happened wouldn't stop him from continuing to live his life that way. Will then broke down and said, "Why don't he want me?" The scene ended in a tear-jerking embrace between Will and his uncle. Gone was the young teen who had never acted before and who mouthed everyone else's lines, and in his place, was Will, the grown man who had several years of acting experience now and who could show emotion, tears, and range. If Hollywood wanted to know whether the real Will Smith could act, all they had to do was watch this powerful, emotional scene.

Over the next two seasons, Will had more opportunities to tackle some tough subjects. In season five's episode "Bullets over Bel-Air," a planned camping trip was cut short for Carlton and Will when a robber approached them at an automated bank teller machine and fired a gun. Will got shot, and the ratings also shot up. However, the writers never completely steered away from *The Fresh Prince's* comedic roots.

HEARTBREAK AND LOVE

The show was doing well, but Will and Jazz's record career was temporarily on hold, and Will's personal life was beginning to suffer. Unfortunately, his marriage to Sheree would be short-lived when the couple realized that they were too young when they married and just weren't in love anymore. They ultimately divorced in 1995. However, looking back on his own parents' marriage and ultimate divorce, Will said he would have stayed together just for the sake of his son: "That's what my parents did. To me, age thirteen felt like an OK time for my parents to say, 'This is not working out.' Thirteen-years-old worked for me. So I would have stayed together until Trey was thirteen and then moved on. Sheree and I didn't have a volatile relationship. It was passive, sort of a drippy faucet. It wasn't fighting, arguing. We never raised our voices. It was . . . Chinese water torture."[16]

The couple's divorce ended with a reported $900,000 lump-sum divorce settlement from Will to Sheree, plus $24,000 per month in alimony and child support for Trey. The divorce, said Will, was the only thing at that point in his life for which he considered himself a failure: "I feel that much more pain, having been divorced. I saw that (with his parents). I saw what that mistake was."[17]

Where Will was not making mistakes, however, was in his career. Up until this point, he had taken roles in movies that did well and that critics enjoyed, but none that were necessarily considered blockbusters, at least according to Hollywood's standards. That would soon change. In 1995, Will teamed up with fellow comedian Martin Lawrence for the movie *Bad Boys*, an action-packed comedy directed by Michael Bay. The movie follows two detectives, Mike Lowery and Marcus Brunette, as they try to find $100 million worth of heroin within 72 hours before Internal Affairs shuts them down.

Will played Michael Lowrey, a police officer with the Miami Police Department, who partners with Marcus Bennett, played by Martin Lawrence. However, the movie wasn't originally written for Martin and Will. Instead, it was originally written for other fellow comedians, Dana Carvey and Jon Lovitz. However, once the director recognized the popularity of both actors (Martin Lawrence had his own successful sitcom, *Martin*, at the time), he signed them as the leads with a $2 million paycheck. After shooting one running scene with Will, cars exploding, Will's shirt open and flapping in the wind, Bay said, "Will, come look at this! This is what a movie star looks like!"[18]

PAYDAY

It's taken a lot for an African American actor to become a star in Hollywood on both the big and small screens. Back in 1950, African American actor and screen legend Sidney Poitier earned only $3,000 for his role in *No Way Out*, and in 1959 he earned $75,000 for *Porgy and Bess*. He was paid $200,000 for both of his movies in the 1960s—*In the Heat of the Night* and *Guess Who's Coming to Dinner*. African American actors still had a long way to go to be paid what other great actors were earning at the time. As an example (although contract stipulations could have varied between actors), Gene Kelly was contracted by MGM at $1,000 per week and later at $2,500 per week.

In the 1990s, things improved when fellow African American actor Denzel Washington received $3 million for *Malcolm X* in 1992. But within the next three years, Washington's salary would explode to a whopping $10 million for his role in the film *Courage Under Fire* in 1995, a movie that grossed $59 million. Could Will one day earn the same commanding salary as Washington? Will moved up in the financial ranks when he was paid $2 million in 1995 for his role in *Bad Boys*. That salary showed he was becoming more respected in Hollywood, but how much higher would he climb?

Will worked hard, earning every bit of his salary, and enjoyed working with Martin. "Martin's hilarious. He's like a machine," said Will. "He's one of the few people I've worked with that you can say go and get something funny in character. It makes me feel like I have to do no work in the scenes. Clean up the slop. Whatever he cleans up in the scene I take that. Every time he opens his mouth, face, delivery, he's just perfection."[19]

However, once again Will had an issue with the filming of a sensitive part of the film (remember the kiss in *Six Degrees of Separation?*). In the *Bad Boys* documentary, director Michael Bay explains that he wanted Will's character to tell Martin's character, "I love you, man" at the end of the movie when both were recovering. Bay said that Will refused, which led to major arguments and an almost complete shutdown of the day's shoot. Bay said that after arguing for hours, Will changed his mind and agreed to say the line.

Lawrence and Smith was a perfect partnership. *Bad Boys* was released April 1995, and the movie that cost $19 million to make grossed $65.8 million in the United States and $141 million worldwide. It became Will's first blockbuster movie. Hollywood is based on numbers, and a great opening weekend for a movie helps to determine the success of an actor. Movies cost millions of dollars to produce, and Hollywood needs to earn back the money that they've spent with a strong opening weekend. The stronger the weekend, the potentially bigger the actor's power. Will made a strong impression on Hollywood that weekend.

However, just because a movie becomes a blockbuster doesn't mean that the critics will love it. "Coherence is not the film's strong suit," wrote Peter Travers of *Rolling Stone* about *Bad Boys*. "Director Michael Bay—the 30-year-old wiz behind commercials and music videos in his feature debut—is out for hip, high-style fun. The climactic shootout inside an airplane hangar, complete with a 727 blowing sky high, slides the film into overdrive. It's all special-effects noise and nonsense. We're not fooled. Lawrence and Smith are the real firecrackers."[20]

Will was a bona fide star in three areas now—television, music, and movies—and headed back to work on the set of *The Fresh Prince of Bel-Air*. It was originally planned to be the last season of the television sitcom, but the cast decided to go one more year. There were some minor changes on the show for this season, including the fact that Jazz was gone from the show and actress Nia Long joined the cast as Will's girlfriend. The show had a lot of guest stars that season, including John Amos, Kareem Abdul-Jabbar, Don Cornelius, Pat Morita, Sherman Hemsley, and more. Underneath it all, though, Will was starting to wonder if it was time to say good-bye to the show.

WILL MEETS JADA

With his movie career on track and the series still doing well, Will focused on getting his personal life together. Will first met Jada in 1990 on his visit to the set of another NBC sitcom, *A Different World*, but he was interested in Sheree at the time. Jada was a petite girl, barely reaching 5 feet in stature. She was an aspiring actress who had just moved from Baltimore, Maryland, to Hollywood with the hopes of having a career. At the time Jada met Will, she was up for the part of Will's girlfriend on *The Fresh Prince of Bel-Air*, but she was passed up for the role. Instead, the part of Lisa Wilkes, Will's girlfriend for 16 episodes, was given to actress Nia Long. It was said that Jada's small stature ultimately held her back as the producers thought she was too short to play opposite the six-foot-two actor.

After the audition, Jada brushed right past Will. "He's like, 'What's up?' and I was like, 'Yeah, how you doing?'" said Jada. "I was ticked off that I didn't get the job."[21] Will and Jada would become friends, but Will's friendship with Jada wouldn't blossom into romance until soon after his divorce from Sheree, a decision Will said he does not regret. "No, we were young, and we have a beautiful baby. So the deal worked out. Everything is cool, and I have a wonderful woman in my life light now," he says.[22]

Jada Pinkett was born September 18, 1971, to Adrienne Banfield-Jones (who got pregnant with Jada while still in high school) and Robsol Pinkett Jr. Adrienne became the head nurse of an inner-city clinic in Baltimore, and Robsol owned a construction company. Jada was named after her mother's favorite soap opera actress, Jada Rowland. Similar to Will's family life, Jada's parents divorced (although after only a few months of marriage). Like Will, Jada also had aspirations of one day being a star. When she was a young girl, her mother signed her up for piano, tap, and ballet lessons. "(My mother) understood what I wanted," said Jada, "and never stood in my way."[23]

Jada was also raised with the help of her grandmother, Marion Banfield, who was employed as a social worker. She was also close to her grandmother, whom she said, "was a doer who wanted to create a better community and add beauty to the world."[24] Jada hoped to do the same one day.

Jada attended the Baltimore School for the Arts, a Baltimore City public high school, with fellow classmate and friend Tupac Shakur. She then packed up and moved to Los Angeles, California, to pursue her acting career. She started her career in a guest role on the sitcom *True Colors* and went on to make appearances in *Doogie Howser, M.D.* and *21 Jump Street*. Then in 1991, Jada won her breakout role playing Lena James on NBC's *A Different World*.

According to the Museum of Broadcast Communications, *A Different World*, which was a spin-off series from *The Cosby Show* developed by comedian Bill Cosby, enjoyed a successful run on NBC from 1987 to 1993. The show was a half-hour, ensemble situation comedy and the first to "immerse America in student life at a historically black college. Over the course of its run, the show was also credited with tackling social and political issues rarely explored in television fiction, and opening doors to the television industry for unprecedented numbers of young black actors, writers, producers and directors."[25] *A Different World* didn't get off to a great start, but it did have a prime-time slot on NBC—

sandwiched between two extremely successful sitcoms, *The Cosby Show* and *Cheers*. After a creative makeover, the show moved up to third and fourth places over the next two seasons and ranked first and second among black viewers.

Jada earned herself positive reviews for her role as Lena, and she was earning a solid reputation as an actress as well. In 1993 she made her feature-film debut in *Menace II Society*, described as an "urban nightmare which chronicles several days in the life of Caine Lawson, following his high-school graduation, as he attempts to escape his violent existence in the projects of Watts, CA."[26] Jada played Ronnie, a young single mother in the gang-riddled neighborhood.

Jada went on to appear in the 1994 movie *The Inkwell*, which follows the adventures of 16-year-old Drew Tate when he spends two weeks with his family and relatives in Martha's Vineyard. Jada played his love interest, Lauren. In 1994, she appeared in both *Jason's Lyric* and *A Low Down Dirty Shame*.

When it came to a relationship with Will, he was once again hesitant when it came to asking a girl out. Although Will was friends with Jada, it took a third party to intervene and move their relationship in a more romantic direction. Actress Tisha Campbell and her husband, Duane Martin, set up Will and Jada on a date, but the two couldn't have been more different. The first obvious difference was their height, at six feet two, Will towered over the small actress. Although Will was a serious man when it came to his career, Jada seemed to have a more serious personality overall. Jada was a strong, independent woman, and Will was a strong, successful man—so it was only a matter of time before they determined whether they were a good match for each other or if they were polar opposites.

Jada seemed more willing to accept the Hollywood lifestyle than Sheree was, and that became an easier match for Will. The couple soon became a regular fixture on the Hollywood circuit. Daphne Reid believed that Jada was a strong woman who wouldn't take b.s. from anyone, even Will Smith.

THE FINAL CURTAIN

After six years on *The Fresh Prince of Bel-Air*, a good run for any sitcom, Will finally decided to call it quits and focus on his movie career.

Will Smith was the type of man who wanted to excel at everything he touched, but he came to the conclusion that his character on the sitcom was becoming a little stale. He wanted to say goodbye to his onscreen character while *The Fresh Prince of Bel-Air* was still considered funny. In addition, Will's movie career was already booming, and he felt that his career was moving more in that direction.

When asked about the show, Will said, "We had a nice run. I did *Six Degrees* and I did *Bad Boys*, and I was working on *Independence Day*, and the television show just felt confining. You're pretty much one character, and there are not many peaks and valleys, just pretty much the same old same old. And I wanted to go out while we were good. You get up to eight or nine seasons and then you're struggling. I wanted to go out solid, while we were still funny."[27]

Over the last six years, audiences watched as Will, *The Fresh Prince* character, grew up on their television screens. When he first arrived at the Banks house from Philadelphia, he was a smart-mouthed teenager who believed his street way was the better way. Throughout the series, Will worked hard in school and learned some valuable lessons along the way. One important lesson was not judging others—for example, his cousin Carlton—the same way he would not want to be judged. He learned how to move on from the rejection of his father and learned how to accept others for who they are, and aren't. He fell in and out, and in and out, of love. He also recognized the importance of a good education. At the end of season five of *The Fresh Prince of Bel-Air*, Will broke up with his fiancé just moments before his wedding. Instead, he returned to Bel-Air and to a college education.

Tatyana Ali, who portrayed young Ashley Banks throughout the entire series, attributed the show's success to the actors and to the writing. "Will's a cutup, but he's one of the smartest young men that I have ever met in this business," she observed. "I think the main key is Will and his charm. For the teen-age audience, I think it's just that we're funny. For the adult audience, it's that our show always has a message, but it's bearable. We don't beat you over the head with it."[28]

The rest of the Banks clan had grown up, too. Carlton was admitted to Princeton University, the college of his dreams, and studied for a career in politics. Hilary had enough life experience to temper her highfalutin, snobbish attitude toward those who didn't have as much as she had. She worked hard and won her own talk show. Ashley, a teen by the end of the show, pursued a singing career. When Hilary's talk show was moved to New York City, Ashley talked her parents into moving with Hilary so that Ashley could attend a performing arts high school. In the finale, the Bel-Air mansion was put up for sale, and the family moved in different directions.

In real life, the cast also moved in different directions. Will Smith grew up, maturing from a teenage rapper who had achieved early success to a full-blown television star who had experienced marriage, divorce, and a new baby along the way. Will moved on to become a major motion picture star and a Hollywood leading man. In 1998, he was chosen by *People* magazine as one of their 50 most beautiful people in the world. Like his fictional counterpart, Will was about to leave the nest—otherwise known as the comfort of filming the weekly sitcom *The Fresh Prince of Bel-Air*—to try the unknown. Will was hoping to move on to even bigger and better things in the movies.

NOTES

1. "The Fresh Prince of Bel-Air." *Entertainment Weekly*. Accessed August 30, 2009. http://www.ew.com/ew/article/0,,310235,00.html.

2. "The Fresh Prince of Bel-Air." *Entertainment Weekly*. Accessed August 30, 2009. http://www.ew.com/ew/article/0,,310235,00.html.

3. "Will Smith's Secret to Success." *Jon Gordon's Blog*. Accessed August 30, 2009. http://www.jongordon.com/blog/2009/06/08/will-smiths-secret-to-success/.

4. "Can Will Smith Play On Park Avenue?" *Entertainment Weekly*. Accessed August 30, 2009. http://www.ew.com/ew/article/0,,309042,00.html.

5. "Will Smith, The Pursuit of Happyness Interview." *UGO.com*. Accessed August 30, 2009. http://www.ugo.com/ugo/html/article/?id=16290.

6. "Will Smith, The Pursuit of Happyness Interview." *UGO.com*. Accessed August 30, 2009. http://www.ugo.com/ugo/html/article/?id=16290.

7. "Can Will Smith Play On Park Avenue?" *Entertainment Weekly*. Accessed August 30, 2009. http://www.ew.com/ew/article/0,,309042,00.html.

8. "Can Will Smith Play On Park Avenue?" *Entertainment Weekly*. Accessed August 30, 2009. http://www.ew.com/ew/article/0,,309042,00.html.

9. Maslin, Janet. "Six Degrees of Separation; John Guare's 'Six Degrees,' on Art and Life Stories, Real and Fake." *The New York Times*. December 8, 1993.

10. Barnet, Megan. "Six Degrees of Separation." *Movie-Vault.com*. Accessed August 30, 2009. http://www.movie-vault.com/reviews/rlLFlgkoUcgaShTt.

11. Norment, Lynn. "Will Smith: On his hot movie career, his divorce, his new lady love and the end of 'The Fresh Prince.'" *BNET*. Accessed August 30, 2009. http://findarticles.com/p/articles/mi_m1077/is_n10_v51/ai_18544351/pg_3?tag=content;col1.

12. "Aunt Viv Dishes It: Will Smith Got Me Fired . . . He Was Too Competitive!!!" *MediaTakeOut.com 2009*. Accessed August 30, 2009. http://www.mediatakeout.com/2009/26107-aunt_viv_dishes_it_will_smith_got_me_fired__he_was_too_competitive.html.

13. "News | Janet Hubert, Will Smith, Fresh Prince, Tell All Book." *Star Magazine*. Accessed September 27, 2009. http://www.starmagazine.com/fresh_prince_mom_janet_tellall_book/news/15735.

14. "Smith, Whitten feud over her 'Fresh Prince' exit—'Fresh Prince of Bel-Air.'" *Jet*. August 30, 1993. Print..

15. Norment, Lynn. "Will Smith: On his hot movie career, his divorce, his new lady love and the end of 'The Fresh Prince.'" *BNET*. Accessed August 30, 2009. http://findarticles.com/p/articles/mi_m1077/is_n10_v51/ai_18544351/pg_3?tag=content;col1.

16. "Cover Story: Will Smith: Love, Paranoia & the Politics of Booty." *Rolling Stone*. Accessed August 30, 2009. http://www.rollingstone.com/artists/willsmith/articles/story/5938077/cover_story_will_smith_love_paranoia__the_politics_of_booty.

17. "Will Smith & Sheree Zampino." *Wed TV*. May 9, 1992. Accessed August 30, 2009. http://www.geocities.com/wedtvsite/celeb_willsshereez.html.

18. *Michael Bay dot com*. http://www.michaelbay.com.

19. *Michael Bay dot com*. http://www.michaelbay.com.

20. "Bad Boys." *Rolling Stone*. Accessed August 30, 2009. http://www.rollingstone.com/reviews/movie/5948199/review/5948200/bad_boys.

21. "Mr. Smith Takes a Bride—Secret Weddings, Jada Pinkett Smith, Will Smith." *People.com*. Accessed August 30, 2009. http://www.people.com/people/archive/article/0,,20124266,00.html.

22. Norment, Lynn. "Will Smith: On his hot movie career, his divorce, his new lady love and the end of 'The Fresh Prince.'" *BNET*. Accessed August 30, 2009. http://findarticles.com/p/articles/mi_m1077/is_n10_v51/ai_18544351/pg_3?tag=content;col1.

23. Keith, Amy Elisa. "Jada Pinkett-Smith: Her Turn." *People Magazine*. April 2, 2007. http://www.people.com/people/archive/article/0,,20061745,00.html.

24. "Jada Pinkett Smith." *VIBE Magazine*. Accessed August 30, 2009. http://www.vibe.com/celebs/about.html?id=184.

25. "Different World." *The Museum of Broadcast Communications*. Accessed August 30, 2009. http://www.museum.tv/archives/etv/D/htmlD/differentwor/differentwor.htm.

26. "Menace II Society Movie Download." *Allmovia.com*. Accessed August 30, 2009. http://www.allmovia.com/mov/menace_ii_society/.

27. Norment, Lynn. "Will Smith: On his hot movie career, his divorce, his new lady love and the end of 'The Fresh Prince.'" *BNET*. Accessed August 30, 2009. http://findarticles.com/p/articles/mi_m1077/is_n10_v51/ai_18544351/pg_3?tag=content;col1.

28. Jackson, Bechetta A. "'Fresh Prince of Bel-Air' Begins Its Fifth Season." *Jet*. September 19, 1994.

Chapter 4

HOLLYWOOD'S GOLDEN BOY

It's not often that you find someone who is great at almost everything he touches. Will was way ahead of other actors trying to make it big in Hollywood. Except for a few little blips on his Hollywood radar screen, Will was succeeding at anything he tried to do in his career. He had a successful music career and television series, and he was at the start of a promising film career.

Will was once asked about the fact that his career had progressed so smoothly, with hardly any obstacles. He told the reporter that it's all about how he views the obstacles and his life that makes him stand out from the crowd: "I've had those (obstacles), but how I view life mellows the undulation. Since you have no control over what life gives you, you have two options: live or kill yourself. And once you decide to live, then my ego kicks in—I'm going to live the best life I possibly can."[1]

Looking back, Will has already overcome a few major obstacles in his short career. He didn't know how to act, yet he became one of the hottest stars in prime-time television. His music with DJ Jazzy Jeff was criticized by other rappers for not being hard core, but their songs sold millions and won many awards. Will earned millions but spent way too much and ended up owing the IRS, yet he paid them back and learned a valuable lesson. His next challenge was to be taken seriously as an actor. Will decided to work hard and overcome these, and other, obstacles.

Will says he was living his life as best as he possibly could, but there was more to his success than just what it did for him. It was also about what Will's success did for Hollywood. Like Sidney Poitier who had opened up doors before him, Will was starting to open his own doors for the next generation. Thanks to this Philly-born rapper's achievements, gone were the days when Hollywood shunned rappers for any roles other than extra gang members in a scene. Instead, rappers were being considered for lead movie and television roles.

After Will's success in *Six Degrees of Separation* and *Bad Boys*, he not only paved his own way to become a major motion-picture star, but he paved the way for other rappers, including Queen Latifah (who guest starred on *The Fresh Prince*; won her own sitcom, *Living Single*, from 1993 to 1998; and then had a successful movie career). Master P produced eight films, wrote and directed six, and starred in over a dozen, including major studio releases such as *Gone in 60 Seconds*, with Nicolas Cage and Angelina Jolie. Busta Rhymes starred in several movies, including *Who's the Man*. LL Cool J and Snoop Doggy Dogg have also appeared in many motion pictures.

While these rappers-turned-actors had decent movie careers, none experienced the same blockbuster success that Will did. Compared to other rappers, Will's success on the big screen would soon leave them in the dust.

"Will used *The Fresh Prince of Bel-Air* as a platform for his personality," said Jason Kaufmann of PopEditor.com. "It's hard to leave a show like that where you carried the show and then go on to a blockbuster career. George Clooney did it when he left *ER* and David Caruso wanted to do it when he left *NYPD Blue*, but it didn't work for him. Stars look at their career as 'it's either movies or nothing,' but Will showed that you can start off very small. Then you can have roles that are tailored to you once you play it off."[2]

WILL'S INDEPENDENCE DAY

Will started off with small roles in movies, and those roles helped him to hone his acting skills. It was at this point in his life, however, that he knew he was ready for bigger, more challenging roles. After directors Dean Devlin and Roland Emmerich watched Will's performance in *Six Degrees of Separation*, they knew that they wanted him for the lead in their sci-fi thriller *Independence Day* (which was also known as ID4). *Independence Day* was about an alien invasion, and Will was cast in the lead role of Captain Steven Hiller, a Marine who is the hero trying to save Earth from the aliens.

The movie earned Will a whopping $5 million paycheck and moved him up a notch on the Hollywood A-list ladder. It was a highly anticipated movie, especially after Fox Broadcasting Company paid more than a million dollars to air a trailer advertising the upcoming movie during Super Bowl XXX. That trailer was incredibly successful, and interest in the movie grew tremendously. The trailer's success enticed other movie production companies to purchase Super Bowl airtime to promote their movies.

The production company for *Independence Day* produced several suspenseful trailers as well as a half-hour special about the movie, all of which worked to whet viewers' desire to see it. The marketing of the movie worked so well that *Independence Day* was screened in some theaters the night before its scheduled release date. Even renowned film director Steven Spielberg told reporters that he was interested in seeing it, "I could never make an evil, aggressive alien movie, but I would sure pay to see one. I'll pay to see this one. Based on the way I think people feel today, I believe *Independence Day* will be the No. 1 film of the year. It will do between $250 million and $300 million, if not more."[3]

Independence Day was released on July 3, 1996, just in time for the very popular Fourth of July movie weekend. In the Hollywood movie industry, those movies released on the Fourth of July weekend are expected to do very well. This holiday weekend often earns the industry millions of dollars in sales. Over the years, many movies have successfully premiered during the Fourth of July weekend, including *Airplane* (1980; earned $83 million worldwide), *Back to the Future* (1985; earned $381 million worldwide), and *Apollo 13* (1995; earned $355 million), just to name a few.

Early reviews for *Independence Day* were very good. "*Independence Day* is the Hollywood version of raising the dead," wrote Kenneth Turan, film critic for *The Los Angeles Times*.[4] "Its frankly spectacular special effects revive a genre that has slept with the fishes since the 1950s, the 'Keep watching the skies' epics of destructive alien invasion. Smith's character is the film's most satisfying. It's to Devlin and Emmerich's credit that they consciously went after an African American for their action hero, and it is nice to see how well that move paid off."[5]

Steven Spielberg took a good guess on the movie's potential earnings, but he wasn't even close. The movie actually earned more than $816 million worldwide—and of that, $104.3 million was in its first week. *Independence Day* was also the highest-grossing film of 1996. The film received, and was nominated for, several awards, including an Academy Award for Visual Effects and an Academy Award nomination for Best Sound. It also received an MTV Movie Award for Best Kiss, a People's Choice Award for Favorite Dramatic Motion Picture, and a Kids' Choice Award for Favorite Movie. The success of *Independence Day* took Will to new heights in Hollywood—the industry that once said to him, "Hey, Will," now addresses him as Mr. Smith.

Will's title might have changed in Hollywood, but he wasn't quite ready to change his title in his personal life, to Mr. and Mrs. Will Smith, just yet. Will was enjoying his movie success and was also thrilled to have such a beautiful woman, Jada Pinkett, on his arm on the red carpet. It was obvious that Will was happy and that he loved her, but after his last matrimonial experience, he wasn't ready to jump into marriage again so fast: "I'm happier than I've been in a while. But I'm not anxious to get married again. I'm speaking from experience. Sometimes you have to get smart and learn from your mistakes."[6]

Will was not just physically attracted to Jada, but he was intellectually attracted to her as well. "She's so intelligent," he said. "She's very in touch with her emotions, which allows me to be in touch with mine. She helps me deal with everything that I have to deal with. She makes everything okay. No matter how difficult it gets, she always has something thing kind to say or a warm hug, or she'll cry with you if you feel like crying. But she'll also punch somebody in the face if they do something to me."[7]

But Jada, a career-oriented woman, wasn't going to sit around waiting for Will to decide when he was ready to propose. She was too busy with her own successful acting career. She already had roles in *The Nutty Professor* with comedian Eddie Murphy; in the 1995 horror film *Tales from the Crypt;* and in the 1996 drama *Set It Off,* as Lita "Stony" Newsom, a movie that also starred rapper Queen Latifah and actress Vivica A. Fox.

Jada also appeared in *If These Walls Could Talk*, a 1996 Golden Globe and Emmy Award–nominated made-for-television movie that follows the stories of three women and their experiences with abortion. Jada also appeared in the horror film *Scream 2*, the next installment in the franchise series. The *Scream* series grossed $172 million.

MEN IN BLACK

It didn't look like anyone could punch a hole in Will's burgeoning movie career at this point—1997 was a banner year for him. He dabbled in every aspect of acting. He lent his voice for the award-winning HBO children's series *Happily Ever After's Pinocchio*, with fellow actors Chris Rock, Charles S. Dutton, and Della Reese.

In addition to developing his career in front of the camera, Will took an interest in expanding his career behind the scenes as well. It was at this time that he founded Overbrook Entertainment, which was named after his high school in Philadelphia, Overbrook High School. Will's goal with this production company was to become more involved in the production end of films.

In the meantime, when it came to the big screen, Will wanted to continue to prove to audiences that he wasn't a one-hit wonder. And all it took was another Fourth of July movie and another $5 million paycheck to have Hollywood buzzing about Will once again. The movie, *Men in Black*, was released on July 2, 1997. Directed by Barry Sonnenfeld, it was an action-packed movie based on the comic book series of the same name.

Will costarred in the feature film with veteran actors Tommy Lee Jones and Vincent D'Onofrio. "I saw Tommy do a TV interview a few years ago, and he was so mean I remember thinking 'Thank God I never have to work with this jerk,'" said Sonnenfeld. "But I ended up loving every minute of it. He can be difficult if you don't have clear opinions, but we got along extraordinarily well."[8]

Men in Black followed the exploits of agents Kay and Jay, members of a top-secret organization established to monitor and police alien activity on Earth. Will played James Edwards, known as Agent J, who is a police officer with the New York Police Department when he is asked to become a member of the MIB, a top-secret agency that monitors alien activity on Earth. Tommy Lee Jones played Agent Kay, a senior MIB agent who recruits and guides Agent Jay. The title *Men in Black* describes the attire they are known for—dark sunglasses and dark suits. The sunglasses were protective shields to protect Kay and Jay from having the device accidentally work on them (Interestingly, the success of the movie lead to an increase in Ray-Ban sales of the Predator 2 sunglasses worn by Will Smith and Tommy Lee Jones. The Ray-Ban sales tripled to almost $5 million.).[9]

Men in Black was spectacular. It was filled with special effects that cost a whopping $90 million to make, but the film grossed more than $587 million worldwide. The success of *Men in Black* gave Will two Fourth-of-July blockbusters in a row. The movie won several awards, including an Academy Award for Best Makeup, and it was nominated for an Academy Award for Best Original Score and Best Art Direction. At the Kids' Choice Awards, *Men in Black* won Favorite Movie, and Will took home the award for Favorite Movie Actor. At the Golden Globes, it was nominated for Best Motion Picture. The critics loved the movie, saying, "Will Smith and Tommy Lee Jones play off each other with unforced, expert timing . . . Taking a cue from Jones, Smith doesn't come off as cocky or in-your-face."[10]

Switching gears, Will wasn't done with his achievements that year. Not wanting to disappoint his music fans, he went back into the studio and recorded another album. He released it on Columbia Records in November. And since it seemed that everything Will did at this point was on a big scale, it was only appropriate to name his first solo album *Big Willie Style*. The album had several hit singles—the first of which was the catchy song "Gettin' Jiggy Wit It."

It was Smith's first hit produced by Poke & Tone, who replaced DJ Jazzy Jeff (although Will and Jazz remained friends). At that year's MTV Awards, "Gettin' Jiggy Wit It" was nominated for best video, best dance video, best choreography, and viewers' choice. Once again, Will took home a Grammy Award in 1999 for best rap solo performance, and "Gettin' Jiggy Wit It" was ranked in the top 100 best songs of the 1990s.

Will released "Men in Black," another single from the album that would also serve as the soundtrack of his hit movie. The third single, "Just the Two of Us," was a cover of the same song written by famed singers Grover Washington Jr. and Bill Withers. Will's version was a combination of the original song combined with his rap message to his real-life five-year-old son Trey, who made a guest appearance in the video. The remainder of the video for the song included clips of celebrity and noncelebrity fathers, including Muhammad Ali, and poignant moments with their children.

Looking back on the career that Will has had, today's music critics understand the crossover appeal—the ability for music to appeal to pop music lovers and rap music lovers—of Will's music. "Will Smith's music paved the way for hip hop being to be able to be commercial," said Tracey Ford. "He has that crossover appeal. The song, 'Getting Jiggy Wit It,' whether or not we consider that song to be corny now, is a commercial concept. It's a slang, but something that was used on (the sitcom) *Will & Grace* and *Ally McBeal*. It's commercial hip hop. Rap artists like Queen Latifah had a much tougher sound than Will did early on, but she's been able to branch out into movies and host award shows. You begin to look at Queen Latifah as a whole separate character, just like Will."[11]

WHAT HAPPENED TO DJ JAZZY JEFF?

Many people wonder what happened to Will's partner DJ Jazzy Jeff after they decided to go their separate ways. DJ Jazzy Jeff didn't disappear into obscurity after *The Fresh Prince of Bel-Air* went off the air and Will's movie career took off. Instead, according to his Web site (http://www.djjazzyjeff.com), he continued on as a successful music producer and founded his own company, A Touch of Jazz, in 2000.

Jazz recorded and produced an album by Jill Scott, a soul singer from Philly, which reached double platinum sales. He continued to work with such artists as Dave Hollister, City High, Floetry, Lil' Kim, and Michael Jackson. Jazz also released a solo album in 2002. The album, called *The Magnificent*, focused on what fans had come to love about Jazz—his ability to scratch. The success of the album brought Jazz back to the touring circuit. In 2004 he released two albums, *Hip Hop Forever II* and *Jazzy Jeff in the House*. In 2005 he and Will finally reunited on Will's album *Lost and Found*.

Lost and Found was Will's fourth solo studio album and his first on Interscope Records after several releases with Columbia Records. Released in early 2005, *Lost and Found* featured the hit single "Switch." Will also had guest artists record on the album, including Mary J. Blige, Snoop Doggy Dog, and Ludacris. Will said that the album's title was based on how he felt lost after putting his music career on hold to do films. Once Will realized that he could do both, he felt like he had found himself again. Interestingly, the art on the cover of the album combined street signs from Will's West Philly roots and his Hollywood career. Like the old days, Jazz produced and scratched on this album.

Music reviewers have said that *Lost and Found* is the closest Will gets to recording a so-called street album. The album included more of Will's humorous songs, which his fans had grown used to, but he also got a little more serious on the album with "I Wish I Made That." The album peaked at number six on the U.S. Billboard Top 200 and was certified Gold by the RIAA on July 6, 2005.

A MARRIED MAN

Time had passed since Will's divorce to Sheree, and his life continued to look good, both professionally and personally. He and Jada had been dating for a few years, and even when Will was away filming his movies, he talked to her all the time. Will was now 29, and he finally realized that he was ready to make a lifetime commitment to Jada, who was 26. He proposed to her in November 1997, and Jada, who once thought that she and Will would never be together when they first met, said yes. Will and Jada tied the knot on New Year's Eve, 1997, with about 100 guests in attendance. The couple had a private ceremony—away from the prying eyes of the paparazzi—that was held at the Cloisters Mansion, a 60-acre estate in Brooklandville, Maryland.

The couple was determined to make their marriage work. After all, Will and Jada's relationship history wasn't chock-full of happily ever afters. Looking back, Will's mom and dad had divorced, Jada's parents had divorced when she was young, and Will's first marriage to Sheree had also ended in divorce. Will and Jada didn't want to make the same mistakes. "With Jada, I stood up in front of God and my family and said, 'till death us do part,'" said Will. "Divorce cannot be an option . . . I honestly believe there is no woman for me but Jada. No-one can handle me the way she does . . . Once you feel someone locked in on you, it's no contest. This is it. I can't imagine what anyone else would offer."[12]

Will knew that having a successful marriage with Jada would take the same kind of commitment that went into making a successful movie, album, or television show. "You got to put in the time," he said. "You got to think about it. You got to ask for help when you need help. You got to conceptualize how you're going to make the next day better than the last day . . . You have to look at it as you look at your work. It's something that's not going to just be there that you can take for granted."[13]

As serious as they are about their relationship, Will and Jada are also a fun-loving couple with a great sense of humor. Jada once said to Will, "You are one of the biggest movie stars in the world. You just sold 8 million albums with your record. You are at the peak of your career and you got married.'" Will replied, "Yeah?" "Jada's reply: "That was just stupid."[14]

Even joking about their relationship, Will knew that marrying Jada wasn't one of the smartest things he had done, but he also knew that he needed something in this relationship that he didn't have in his relationship with Sheree. Will remembered a look his grandmother gave him when he was growing up, a look that he ached for after his teenage girlfriend cheated on him. "(There was) a look in her eyes that said how much she loved me," said Will. "I need my wife and the women in my life to look at me like that. I just want the women in my world to think that I am a real king."[15]

NOTES

1. "Will Smith: Love, Paranoia & the Politics of Booty." *Rolling Stone*. Accessed August 30, 2009. http://www.rollingstone.com/artists/willsmith/articles/story/5938077/cover_story_will_smith_love_paranoia__the_politics_of_booty.

2. Jason Kaufmann, interview with author, June 30, 2009.

3. Corliss, Richard. "The Invasion Has Begun!" *Time magazine*. July 8, 1996.

4. "Independence Day—Movie Review." *Los Angeles Times*. Accessed August 30, 2009. http://www.calendarlive.com/movies/reviews/cl-movie960716-1,2,1312906.story.

5. "Independence Day—Movie Review." *Los Angeles Times*. Accessed August 30, 2009. http://www.calendarlive.com/movies/reviews/cl-movie960716-1,2,1312906.story.

6. "Mr. Smith Goes To War Will's High-Tech When He's Battling Aliens In New Movie—But Low-Key When He's Being Himself." *NY Daily News*.

Accessed August 30, 2009. http://www.nydailynews.com/archives/entertain ment/1996/06/30/1996-06-30_mr__smith_goes_to_war_will_s.html.

7. Norment, Lynn. "Will Smith: On his hot movie career, his divorce, his new lady love and the end of 'The Fresh Prince.'" *BNET*. Accessed August 30, 2009. http://findarticles.com/p/articles/mi_m1077/is_n10_v51/ai_ 18544351/pg_3?tag=content;col1.

8. "Men in Black." *Entertainment Weekly*. Accessed August 30, 2009. http://www.ew.com/ew/article/0,,287928,00.htm.

9. "And Now a Word From Our Sponsor | Teachable Moment." *Media Awareness Network*. Accessed August 30, 2009. http://www.media-awareness. ca/english/resources/educational/teachable_moments/word_from_our_sponsor.cfm.

10. "Men In Black." *Salon.com*. Accessed August 30, 2009. http://www. salon.com/july97/entertainment/mib970704.html.

11. Tracey Ford, interview with the author, June 30, 2009.

12. "Will Smith & Jada Pinkett Smith—Relationship Details." *FamousHook ups.com*. Accessed August 30, 2009. http://www.famoushookups.com/site/rela tionship_detail.php?name=Will-Smith&celebid=648&relid=119.

13. "Who Scares Will Smith?" *CBS News*. Accessed August 30, 2009. http:// www.cbsnews.com/stories/1998/11/19/archive/main23038.shtml?source=search_ story.

14. Moody, Nekesa M. "Will Smith's Star Continues To Rise With 'Enemy of the State.'" *La Prensa San Diego*. December 11, 1998. Accessed August 30, 2009. http://www.laprensa-sandiego.org/archieve/december11/star.htm.

15. "Will Smith Chucks the Gags." *The Nation*. December 15, 2007. Accessed August 30, 2009. http://www.nationmultimedia.com/2007/12/15/life style/lifestyle_30059147.php.

Chapter 5

THE $20 MILLION MAN

With two Oscar nominations and almost four and a half billion dollars in box office to his credit, a movie starring Will Smith is about as close as you can get to having a sure thing, whether it's science-fiction, romantic comedy, or summer blockbuster.

—*60 Minutes*

Hollywood started calling it "Big Willie Weekend," and there was good reason. Will Smith seemed to own the Hollywood movie box office on the Fourth of July weekend. He really owned it for the last two years with the release of *Independence Day* and *Men in Black,* and moviegoers around the globe were anxious to see what Will was going to do next. While Will was filming his next possible blockbuster, he was also busy expanding his family. In true Big Willie style, his first child with Jada arrived around the Fourth of July in 1998. Jada and Will became proud parents to Jaden Christopher Syre Smith, born July 8 and weighing seven pounds one ounce. Jaden was the second son for Will and the first child for Jada.

The relationship between Jada and Will was obviously a strong one, and they were slowly emerging as a Hollywood power couple. A power couple is one in which both individuals have high-powered careers or are politically influential. It was obvious that Will fit the description, and Jada was busy with her own solo career.

But although Jada had a successful movie year prior to the couple's wedding, when Jaden came along, it was apparent that the new parents would need time to figure out how to balance both careers. Jada knew, however, with the birth of their first child, that her career as a mother was just as important—if not more important—than her own movie and television career. Jada had career dreams of her own, and they were just as big as those that Will had, but she also recognized that Will's rise to fame and fortune at this point was unstoppable. So Jada recognized the need to sacrifice a bit in her career to be there while Will's career kept moving forward.

"When I came to Hollywood, I planned on being the biggest star," said Jada, "but when I got with Will, I said, 'I'm going to have to compromise, because he's not going to. That's not even a discussion.' So I had to ask myself, 'Is career more important than having a good man who loves you and will provide a happy family?' I choose Will. So now my work gets forty percent. I can still have a career. I just won't have the one I planned on. That will not happen. I put my family first."[1]

Will is also a dedicated family man, but even the newlywed and second-time dad didn't slow down when it came to his career. He was set on becoming the biggest movie sensation, and he worked extremely hard at choosing the right projects. In November 1998, Will's next movie, *Enemy of the State*, was released, costarring Gene Hackman, Jon Voight, Lisa Bonet, and Regina King. The movie was produced by Jerry Bruckheimer, who had worked with Will previously on the movie *Bad Boys*. The story focuses on Robert Clayton Dean, played by Will, who is a lawyer that becomes the target of a corrupt politician and his NSA goons when he accidentally, and unknowingly, receives key evidence to a serious politically motivated crime.

Will almost tripled his last paycheck for this film, earning a whopping $14 million, but a large paycheck still didn't guarantee to Hollywood that Will was worth it. The *Los Angeles Times* called Will's performance convincing: "To do that a film has to have convincing performers, and this one demonstrates why Will Smith is pretty much the hottest actor in Hollywood. As Robert Clayton Dean, the man unjustly placed at the top of the NSA's bad list, Smith adds dramatic skills to his comic gifts and his immense relaxed likability and ends up as everyone's favorite Everyman, in a jam but determined to get out alive."[2]

The movie *Enemy of the State* was a fast-paced movie with chase scene after chase scene, and it did extremely well with worldwide audiences. *Enemy of the State* grossed over $250 million, and although it wasn't the number one movie of the weekend when it debuted, it was still considered a serious success. The 31-year-old Will had finally proved to Hollywood that he was fast becoming the hottest actor in Hollywood. However, even the biggest stars wonder how much longer their popularity and success can last. Will had a string of successes in music, television, and movies, but could it possibly last? Was there a flop soon in his future?

THE GOLDEN BOY SLIPS

In 1999, Will had a cameo role in director Spike Jones' *Torrance Rises*, a mockumentary based on a dance group in Torrance, California, in which he traces their journey to the *MTV Video Music Awards* presentation. But Hollywood had its eyes more on Will's next feature film, for which he donned a cowboy hat and boots. It was a remake of the original television show *Wild, Wild West*, a science-fiction western that ran on CBS from 1965 to 1969.

The main character, Captain James West, was portrayed by veteran actor Robert Conrad. The show told the story of two Secret Service agents—West and Artemus Gordon. Their job was to protect the president and the United States. Robert Conrad was vocal about his displeasure with *Wild, Wild West*. His complaints surrounded the fact that the show is set in the late 1800s. This was at a time when a black man would not have been allowed to be a Secret Service agent. It was also developed at a time where casting a black actor in Conrad's lead part wouldn't have been allowed. *Men in Black*'s director, Barry Sonnenfield, also took several other liberties with the movie, irritating Conrad.

The film version of *Wild, Wild West* costarred Kevin Kline, Kenneth Branagh, and Salma Hayek. It was released during the Fourth of July weekend, but this movie was much different than those Will had appeared in before. *Wild, Wild West* didn't have aliens or big extravaganza special effects and Will knew that audiences were going to be expecting that from him. Even still, Will believed in the movie, and it was a chance that Big Willie was prepared to take. Will even took a smaller paycheck for the film—receiving only $7 million.

Unfortunately, taking a gamble doesn't always pay off. *Wild, Wild West* became one of the few big flops in Will's movie screen career. The movie took a bad hit from the critics, who called it a "noisy, joyless, bizarrely static fiasco."[3] It even received three Razzie Awards, which are given out for the worst movies of the year. Although the movie seemed to start out pretty well, earning $49.7 million in its first week, it ended up only making $222 million worldwide. While that figure might sound good for other movies, *Wild, Wild West* actually cost a whopping $170 million to produce, leaving it with very little profit. Therefore, based on the numbers that the production company needed and was hoping for, it was considered a huge disappointment in comparison to the success of Will's previous summer blockbusters. For the first time, Will had flopped, and flopped big, at the box office.

About a decade later, when he was promoting another movie, *Hancock*, Will apologized publicly to actor Robert Conrad. Will told Conrad that he was sorry for the poor results from the movie and that changing it perhaps wasn't a good idea: "Hancock may not be your favorite (movie), but hopefully, other than *Wild, Wild West*, it's not the worst movie you've ever seen. I made a mistake on *Wild, Wild West*. That could have been better . . . No, it's funny because I could never understand why Robert Conrad was so upset with *Wild, Wild West*. And now I get it. It's like, 'That's my baby! I put my blood, sweat and tears into that!' So I'm going to apologize to Mr. Conrad for that because I didn't realize. I was young and immature. So much pain and joy went into *The Fresh Prince* that my greatest desire would be that it's left alone. But I'm sure some kid someday is going to be fantastic and it's going to be bigger than it was with me. And I'm going to be angry [laughs]."[4]

Wild, Wild West might not have been another number one hit at the box office for Will, but he was already focusing on his next album. He had released *Willennium*, his second solo album, which produced a new string of hit rap singles. The first single, "Wild, Wild West," the song that served as the soundtrack for the movie, featured Alfonso Riberio, Will's costar from *The Fresh Prince of Bel-Air*. It became a number one hit on July 24, 1999. The next single was "Will 2K," a song about New Year's Eve, 1999.

Unfortunately, Will experienced a double whammy in a short period of time—not only did *Wild, Wild West* fail to meet box-office expectations, but *Willenium* also failed to meet commercial success in the music industry. Of course, selling four million copies of any record is otherwise considered a success, but when your name is Will Smith and your other albums have done considerably better, this is a disappointment. The album didn't reach number one on any of the music charts, although it did make it to number five on the U.S. charts. It was beat out by albums from Korn, fellow rapper Dr. Dre, and singer Celine Dion. Once New Year's Eve passed, the album dropped even further, and by June 2000 it disappeared completely off the charts. Once again, Hollywood's golden boy was slipping just a little, and Hollywood wondered how much further he would fall.

Falling out of favor with audiences has happened to other megastars— a few bad movie choices, and they lose their star power. Take actor John Travolta, for example. His breakout role was in the hit television sitcom *Welcome Back Kotter* in the late 1970s. Based on his success and the popularity of that show, he was given movie roles in the Steven King horror flick *Carrie* and in the drama *The Boy in the Plastic Bubble*. He even released a single, "Let Her In" that hit the Billboard Hot 100 chart. Travolta then landed the lead in blockbuster movies such as *Saturday Night Fever* (1977) and *Grease* (1978). He received an Academy Award nomination for *Saturday Night Fever* and then had the lead in the hit film *Urban Cowboy*. Travolta was having a successful run, and it seemed that nothing could take him down. Unfortunately, his star power started to fade after several of his next movies—*Staying Alive, Perfect,* and *Two of a Kind*—were box-office flops. John disappeared from Hollywood, and it took him years to recover. When director Quentin Tarantino offered him a role in his movie *Pulp Fiction*, Travolta accepted and received fantastic reviews for his performance. That movie brought him back onto Hollywood's radar and eventually back to A-list status.

Was Will's career starting to go in the same direction as John Travolta's had? And, if so, would Will be able to recover? On October 31, 2000, Will and Jada welcomed their second child together, daughter Willow Camille Reign Smith. The Smith family was growing, and, regardless of his last movie, Will was still in demand and busy working on his career. With his next movie, he was going to move in a different creative direction. *The Legend of Bagger Vance* was directed by the legendary actor and director Robert Redford and was based on the novel of the same name by Stephen Pressfield.

The Legend of Bagger Vance was set in the 1930s, and Will played Bagger Vance. Junuh, played by Matt Damon, is a promising golfer who fought in World War I and was traumatized by the experience. When Junuh returns to his hometown in Savannah, Georgia, he is a drunk and an outcast. When an exhibition golf match is scheduled between golf pros Bobby Jones and Walter Hagen, Junuh is asked to join to draw local interest. Bagger Vance becomes his caddy and helps him overcome his fears and play golf again. The movie is much deeper and more thought-provoking than Will's previous movies and the critics called Will "likable and witty as the colloquially wise vagabond shaman who saves the day—and the movie—from otherwise certain grief."[5]

The film was released in November 2000, and although Will received good reviews of his performance, the film itself was yet another financial loss at the box office. *The Legend of Bagger Vance* had a $60 million production budget, but it only garnered $38 million in ticket sales. Was Will's success streak over, or was he only going to be successful with movies that had special effects and that involved fighting aliens? Was that all the audiences wanted to see from him? Hollywood insiders were starting to wonder, but Will didn't seem worried at all.

I AM THE CHAMPION

When Will was born in September 1968, Muhammad Ali was already a 26-year-old champion boxer. Muhammad Ali, born Cassius Clay Jr. began his boxing career by winning a gold medal in the Olympics light heavyweight division. He went on to win the heavyweight championship fights three times and in 1999 was named Sportsman of the Year. As a young rapper, Will was so impressed with the champ that he referred to Ali and his poetic smack talk—such as, "I am the Champ!"—in several of his rap videos. Will admired Ali, but it wasn't until he starred in *The Fresh Prince of Bel-Air* that he first heard his own name associated with that of the ex-heavyweight champ. It was in 1992, when Ali's daughter Maryum, an aspiring musician who lived in Philadelphia with Ali's second wife Khalilah after their divorce, suggested to Will that he play the part of her father in a movie about his life.

So with all this admiration, it seemed only natural that Will would want to play the part of the boxing icon in the biographical film *Ali*, directed by Michael Mann. But he initially had to turn the part down. He was in the middle of filming *The Legend of Bagger Vance*. However, after a behind-the-scenes production delay on *Ali*, the producers returned to offer the lead part to Will once again, and this time it was accompanied with a $20 million paycheck. Will took the part.

$20 MILLION PAYCHECK

Hollywood success can be measured in different ways. First, if it's measured by how well an actor fills seats in movie theaters, then Will was already successful before the movie *Ali* ever hit the movie screen. Second, if success in Hollywood is measured by box-office receipts, then Will Smith was, once again, successful even before the release of *Ali*. Third, if success is measured by the size of a star's paycheck, then Will Smith hit the trifecta with *Ali*.

A $20 million per-movie paycheck is rare in Hollywood, so when Will earned this sum for *Ali*, it put him in a select A-list category with other film superstars. Jim Carrey earned $350,000 for *Ace Ventura, Pet Detective* in 1994 and two years later was paid $20 million for *The Cable Guy*. Kevin Costner, considered an A-list star, earned $14 million for *Waterworld* in 1995, while Mel Gibson received $12 million for *Lethal Weapon 3* in 1992, $15 million for *Maverick* in 1994, and $20 million for *Ransom* in 1996. Other movie actors, such as Arnold Schwarzenegger, Sylvester Stallone, and Bruce Willis were also earning between $15 million and $25 million per movie.

The only other African American actor to pull in a hefty paycheck like Will's at the time was Eddie Murphy who made $15 million for *Beverly Hills Cop III* in 1994, $12 million for *The Nutty Professor* in 1996, and $17 million for *Doctor Dolittle* in 1998. It was obvious that Will had climbed to the top of the ladder. Hollywood expected a lot from him, and he was ready to prove that he could match or surpass what the other veteran actors were doing.

Will threw himself into the role of Ali, preparing both mentally and physically to look and sound just like the great fighter. Will studied Islam, Ali's religion, and took voice lessons to speak more like him. He trained hard in the gym for a year, working with fitness trainers Darryl Foster and Angelo Dundee (who trained Ali in real life). He gained 20 pounds and a lot of muscle, and he developed very realistic boxing skills. To practice his boxing skills, Will would spar with another legendary real-life fighter, Sugar Ray Leonard. Will said that Muhammad Ali, nicknamed "The Great One" in the sports world, would come to the gym to check on Will's progress. Will wanted the film and the fight scenes to look as realistic as possible, so he would actually take blows to the face and body by actor Charles Shufford, who played boxer George Foreman.

Ali didn't open on the Fourth of July, but it did open on Christmas Day, December 25, 2001. It grossed a total of $14.7 million on its opening weekend and a total of $87.7 million worldwide. Will received good reviews for his performance, including one positive review by famed movie critic Roger Ebert, who didn't seem to like the movie as a whole but wrote of Will's performance, "This is despite what is actually a good job of acting by Will Smith in the title role. He has bulked up and looks convincing in the ring, but the key element of his performance is in capturing Ali's enigmatic, improvisational personality. He gets the soft-spoken, kidding quality just right, and we sense Ali as a man who plays a colorful public role while keeping a private reserve. There are times when he grows distant from even those close to him, and they look at him as if into a mystery. The real problem with Smith's performance is the movie it finds itself in. Smith is the right actor for Ali, but this is the wrong movie. Smith is sharp, fast, funny, like the Ali of trash-talking fame, but the movie doesn't unleash that side of him, or his character."[6]

Ebert might not have thought *Ali* was the right movie for Will, but the Academy of Motion Pictures Arts and Sciences saw something great in Will's performance. On Tuesday, February 12, 2002, at 5:30 A.M., Will learned that he was nominated for his first Academy Award. He was thrilled. "My life as an actor has changed forever because now people will always say Oscar-nominated Will Smith," exclaimed the actor. "That's gravy. You can never take that away from me."[7] It was also the first time in Academy Award history that two black men—the other being Denzel Washington for *Training Day*—were nominated in the best actor category.

So, now it's March 24, 2002, and 33-year-old Will Smith sits in the Kodak Theater in Hollywood, California, with his wife Jada Pinkett

Smith. The *74th Annual Academy Awards* show—more commonly known as the Oscars—is underway, and Will is about to find out if he's won the Best Actor in a Leading Role for his portrayal of the legendary boxer Muhammad Ali in the film *Ali*. Unfortunately, when the winner's name is called, it's not Will Smith. Instead, the award is given to Denzel Washington.

However, even with a $20 million paycheck and an Academy Award nomination, Will still isn't convinced that he's as talented as some of the other A-list stars in Hollywood. Remember, when Will does something, he wants to do it right and never be "not good enough" again. If he feels that his acting job wasn't good enough, he'll do something to improve. So when he lost the Academy Award to Washington, Will thought that he needed to work harder on his dramatic acting skills acting, so he could be better. As a result, he hired acting coach Aaron Speiser, who has trained and coached actors for over 25 years, including Jennifer Lopez, LL Cool J, Brooke Shields, and more.

"Will didn't understand what happened with *Ali*," said Speiser. "He works harder than anyone, but he wanted to be better."[8] Speiser knew that Will hadn't had any formal acting training prior to his role on *The Fresh Prince of Bel-Air*. Much of what Will knew about acting came naturally, and the rest he learned through his on-the-job experience working on various movies and television shows. Speiser said that what Will needed to be taught at that point was finding the deep, raw emotion in a character.

"I taught him that acting is creating life, living, it's an imaginary world of the script, it's the end point moving toward these words," Speiser said. "He had to find out where the world is coming from, not just memorizing the world. Year by year, he started to explore his imagination and life experiences and bringing that into his work. The older you get the more you can use your imagination."[9]

Speiser said that there weren't any bad acting habits to break Will of and that he really was a natural in front of the camera. "I added to what he already knew him and taught him how to bring real pain to the characters," he said. "He wasn't looking for the pain. You have to look for it and it has to be mined, sculpted and focused into the character. It's different for men to show emotion."[10]

Will stored what Speiser taught him in the back of his mind, but Will's next film returned him to the special-effects, alien-fighting, blockbuster movie genre. *Men in Black II*, also known as MIIB, was a sequel to the first *Men in Black* movie and jammed packed with special effects and new aliens, not exactly the *Ali* -style of acting. Will teamed up again with Tommy Lee Jones, as well as Lara Flynn Boyle, Johnny Knoxville, Rosario Dawson, and Rip Torn. The production company had to refilm the ending, which was originally scheduled to take place at the World Trade Center in New York City, but because of the September 11, 2001, terrorist attacks on New York City, it had to be moved to a new location.

Recognizing the profit from the first *Men in Black* movie, Will not only signed on for his second $20 million paycheck, but he also signed a contract to receive 10 percent of the film's gross revenue. *Men in Black II* became yet another of Will's Fourth of July blockbusters. It was released on July 3, 2002. Those extra contract bonuses proved to be an extremely smart business move for Will. The movie was a huge commercial success, grossing more than $52 million its first weekend and a total of more than $441 million worldwide. Although there has not been any formal announcement of another *Men in Black* sequel, it is rumored to be in the works. On September 28, 2008, producer Walter Parke told *Personality Parade* magazine "the challenge is getting the script right and finding a time when our busy stars are available . . . Everyone, including Will Smith and Tommy Lee Jones, wants to do another."[11]

The Golden Boy was back at the top of Hollywood's helm, succeeding at what he did so well—the formula action-packed movie. Once again, he was Hollywood's summer blockbuster moneymaker, and he was a well-paid A-list star. However, now that Will was in his mid-30s, and even though he succeeded with *Men in Black II*, he wondered if he would be able to keep up the pace of this one-movie-a-year routine. Would he be able to keep up the same financial success for much longer, or would audiences tire of him?

ALL IN THE FAMILY

Will worked hard to take care of his family's needs. When he was young and lived in West Philadelphia in the 1970s, the average price of a home was $45,000. When Will and Jada moved to Calabasas, California, the Hollywood power couple purchased and renovated a $20 million castle that they called home for themselves and their three children (Will's son from his first marriage visited often). Calabasas, California, is a city within Los Angeles County, California, and is home to many celebrities, including rocker Tommy Lee and actress Melissa Gilbert from *Little House on the Prairie*. The castle is on 20 acres and comes with it's own lake—a lake that Will named after Jada—as well as full-sized basketball and tennis courts.

Will supports his family both financially and emotionally and that means supporting his wife and children's career choices as well. It was already obvious that Jada, his wife of three years now, was a talented, successful woman who was enjoying her own successes on the big screen. Like Will, Jada branched out from her movie and television career as well, launching her own music career in 2002 as founder of the metal rock band Wicked Wisdom, for which she is a singer and songwriter. She formed the band back in 1999 and chose to sing the heavy-metal music that she loved.

"It may be surprising to some but I have always listened to Black Sabbath, Ozzy and Guns N' Roses, and my aunt and uncle loved Queen, Led Zeppelin and The Who as well as reggae and jazz. I come from a very eclectic musical background," said Jada.[12] As many new bands do, Wicked Wisdom[13] started with performances in small local bars. They got their big break when they opened for pop singer Britney Spears on her European tour in 2005 and were able to promote their debut album, *My Story*. The album's sound was very dark and rough, a sound that many of Jada's fans might not have expected from her.

In 2005, Wicked Wisdom performed at Ozzfest, an annual festival tour of the United States featuring performances by many heavy-metal and hard-rock bands. Unfortunately, having the last name of Smith and a husband who had an extremely successful music career didn't guarantee success for Jada. She hit some rough roads, especially during Ozzfest when attendees were angered by Wicked Wisdom's appearance and questioned the group's true heavy-metal abilities. According to some reports, angered fans even filled online message boards and the Ozzfest Web sites with death threats and talk of riots.[14] The group even faced enraged attendees who threw water bottles at them and demanded that the band leave. It was reported that Jada and her group had to cut some sets short.

"The first six shows were really rough. We had a steep learning curve," said Jada. "Those first few shows, the fans were brutal. By the time we got to show No. 7 the audience started to come around. By the end of the tour, during our last set, we had three mosh pits going while we were playing. The crowd was truly with us."[15]

Jada and Will are two very determined people, and they will work hard to achieve whatever they want to achieve. Jada is a keen business-woman. She has worked hard to represent herself as an independent woman, separate from Will Smith, who has her own career as an actress, songwriter, singer, and producer. She founded her own production company, 100% Women Productions, and works on movie and television projects. She dabbled in other areas as well, including designing her own clothing line. She was also proud of the fact that she was a mom of two and a stepmom to one, and in 2004 she became an author of a children's photo essay book entitled *We Girls Hold Up This World* (Cartwheel Publishers).

When discussing her reasoning for writing this self-empowering book for girls, Jada admitted that she was disturbed when Jaden, Will's son from his first marriage, told her that he thought a "fly" girl had to have "a flat stomach, big breasts and a short skirt." She told him, "Let's talk about that, because I have a few things I want to say."[16]

Jada also worked in voice-overs, lending her voice to a very popular computer-animated film, *Madagascar*, produced by DreamWorks Animation. It was released on May 27, 2005, and focuses on four Central Park Zoo animals who are unexpectedly shipped back to Africa but on the way get shipwrecked on the island of Madagascar. Jada is the voice of Gloria the Hippo, the character who takes care of others. Jada and Will's daughter, Willow, was the voice of the young Gloria. Jada also appeared in *The Matrix Reloaded*, a 2003 film and the second installment of the *Matrix* trilogy, with Keanu Reeves. Jada portrayed Captain Niobe. *The Matrix Reloaded* pulled in more than $738 million at the box office.

"I'm one of those people who like to do 100 things at once," she said. "So I'm trying to focus on one. It's a hard thing, because I'm a creative person and I'm constantly coming up with new ideas and find it hard to put anything on the backburner."[17]

It was only a matter of time before Will and Jada combined their talents and drive to become cowriters and producers on various projects. Of course, it made sense that the couple would start by producing a story about a topic that was near and dear to their hearts—their own interesting, mixed-family lives. Will and Jada created, wrote, and produced the half-hour sitcom *All of Us*, through their Overbrook Entertainment company.

All of Us was a comedy about an entertainment reporter and divorcee raising his son (Bobby Jr.) with his ex-wife (Neesee) while also dating a kindergarten teacher (Tia). *All of Us* was eerily similar to Will's life of raising his first son Trey with his ex-wife Sheree, while also being married to Jada and raising Jaden and Willow. Jada pitched the comedy idea to the networks, but she soon learned that being a celebrity doesn't guarantee an approval for a television show, nor does it automatically make that show successful. Les Moonves, chairman of CBS, once said, "Ultimately, America doesn't care who's behind the camera if the show isn't good."[18]

Jada was finally able to sell the show idea to the UPN network where it debuted on September 16, 2003. Occasionally, Will and Jada's real-life son Jaden, who was a mere six years old at the time, appeared in a few episodes. It was Jaden's first taste of acting, and it seemed to come naturally to the curly haired boy.

Will loves being a father and has always supported his children's choices, even as they decide whether they want to follow in his and Jada's footsteps. At home, when he's disciplining the kids, he reaches back into what his military father taught him during his own childhood. Will admitted that his dad was strict—and very particular about things, even forcing him and his brother and sisters to make hospital corners on their beds—but wanted to instill some of that discipline into his own children. "I want my kids to be disciplined and focused, so I try to be a tough dad, but Trey is so hilarious, it cracks me up," said Will.[19]

While Jada and Will were working on the premier of *All of Us*, Will also had the premier of his second movie sequel, *Bad Boys II*, another action-comedy film, directed by Michael Bay and produced by Jerry Bruckheimer. *Bad Boys II* wasn't released on a Fourth of July weekend, but it was released two weeks later on July 18, 2003. Yet the movie still impressed audiences and earned $273 million worldwide, which was more in box-office sales than the original movie had made. *Bad Boys II* was nominated for Best Action Sequence at the *MTV Movie Awards*.

Will loved working on the *Bad Boys* films and said he would make more of them if he could. "Let me tell you, I would do up to *Bad Boys 6* if I could," said Will. "I have so much fun working with Martin Lawrence. I love Miami. It's like that little boy fantasy with fast cars and girls and I got the gun and the bad guys always lose. It's like I would make *Bad Boys* forever."[20]

The series premier of *All of Us* did well in the ratings, but in the following weeks it lost a little bit of steam. *All of Us* eventually settled down and held its own in the ratings on the UPN network for a couple of years but was cancelled at the end of the 2005–06 season. It was then picked up on the CW network for the fall of 2006. *All of Us* struggled after being shifted between the Sunday and Monday night time slots, but once again, it settled in comfortably for a year on Monday nights. It became the CW's fourth most-watched sitcom. Unfortunately, however, its success on the new network didn't parlay into overall television ratings throughout the year, and the show was ultimately cancelled in May 2007.

All of Us did receive several accolades, including nominations from the BET Comedy Awards for Outstanding Director (Debbie Allen and *The Fresh Prince's* Alfonso Ribeiro), Outstanding Lead Actor, Outstanding Supporting Actor and Actress, Outstanding Writing, and several nominations from the Image Awards, including Outstanding Comedy Series, Actor, Supporting Actress, and Writing.

Who knows how Will did it all and managed to keep a happy family and home life, but he still continued to crank out a movie year after year. In 2004, he changed gears and worked on another animated comedy film, lending his voice to the lead character in DreamWorks Animation's *Shark Tale*. Will provided the voice for Oscar, a young fish who claims to have killed the shark mob's son in order to make himself look good in the community. Unfortunately, the movie came out only a year after competitor Pixar's blockbuster movie *Finding Nemo*, an Academy Award–winning animated movie that grossed over $864 million worldwide. The comparisons to both movies were there, but from a critical standpoint, *Finding Nemo* beat the competition. However, *Shark Tale* still debuted at number one in its opening week, and it grossed more than $47 million. Overall, the film took in more than $367 million worldwide.

With the success of *Bad Boys II* and *Shark Tale*, Will seemed to be back on track—he was drawing audiences to the movies and bringing in millions at the box office. For his next movie, he already had success battling aliens, and he was going to see if audiences would want to watch him fight robots in *I, Robot*. *I, Robot* was a science-fiction film set in the year 2035 and was based on nine short stories told by famous science-fiction writer Isaac Asimov in which humans and robots interact with one another. The movie once again lined up with Will's formula for a hit motion picture—it had villains, fights, explosions, and more. But its connection to science connected personally with Will, who as a young student enjoyed his science classes and dreamed of one day being a scientist. "When I got to be 11- or 12-years-old I got interested in entertainment. So being in a sci-fi film is a perfect blend of the two," he said.[21]

Since *I, Robot* fit Will's formula of a successful movie, he received an incredible $28 million salary because it was almost a guaranteed moneymaker. When the movie was released on July 16, 2004, *I, Robot* earned more than $345 worldwide, and Will once still the reigning king of the sci-fi blockbuster. "He's one of the last true leading men," said Alex Proyas, who directed Will in *I, Robot*. "There's a connection he has with audiences who will see him in anything he does. I don't quite know how you explain that kind of magic."[22]

NOTES

1. "Will Smith: Love, Paranoia & the Politics of Booty: Will Smith : Rolling Stone." *Rolling Stone*. Accessed August 30, 2009. http://www.rollingstone.com/artists/willsmith/articles/story/5938077/cover_story_will_smith_love_paranoia__the_politics_of_booty

2. Kenneth Turan, "Enemy of the State, 'Enemy' Has a Little Secret: Let the (Nifty) Chase Begin," *Los Angeles Times*. November 20, 1998.

3. "Wild Wild West | Movie Review." *Entertainment Weekly*. Accessed August 30, 2009. http://www.ew.com/ew/article/0,,272269,00.html.

4. O'Toole, Lesley. "The Total Film Interview." *Total Film*. February 2009, pp. 120–25.

5. "The Legend of Bagger Vance Movie Review, DVD Release." *Filmcritic.com.* Accessed August 30, 2009.<http://www.filmcritic.com/misc/emporium.nsf/reviews/The-Legend-of-Bagger-Vance.

6. Ebert, Roger. *Roger Ebert's Movie Yearbook 2004.* Grand Rapids, MI: Andrews McMeel, 2003.

7. "Academy Announces Oscar Nominations." *FilmStew.Com.* Accessed August 30, 2009. http://www.filmstew.com/showArticle.aspx?ContentID=2586.

8. Aaron Speiser, interview with the author, June 29, 2009.

9. Aaron Speiser, interview with the author, June 29, 2009.

10. Aaron Speiser, interview with the author, June 29, 2009.

11. "Personality Parade." *PARADE Magazine.* Accessed August 30, 2009. http://www.parade.com/celebrity/2008/09/personality-parade-stars-with-stubble.

12. "Metal Bands—Wicked Wisdom." *Metal Underground.com.* Accessed August 30, 2009. http://www.metalunderground.com/bands/details.cfm?bandid=3126.

13. "Wicked Wisdom Frontwoman Interview." *Ultimate-Guitar.com.* Accessed August 30, 2009. http://www.ultimate-guitar.com/news/interviews/wicked_wisdom_frontwoman_interview.html.

14. Mcneill, Darrell M. "Navigating the Metal Minefield: Race, Gender, Celebrity & Headbangers: Wicked Wisdom in the Ozzfest Moshpit." *Creative Loafing Charlotte.* August 31, 2005. Accessed August 30, 2009. http://charlotte.creativeloafing.com/gyrobase/PrintFriendly?oid=125507

15. "Wicked Wisdom Frontwoman Interview." *Ultimate-Guitar.com.* Accessed August 30, 2009. http://www.ultimate-guitar.com/news/interviews/wicked_wisdom_frontwoman_interview.html.

16. "Jada pens children's book." *BreakingNews.ie.* Accessed August 30, 2009. http://www.breakingnews.ie/entertainment/kfgbeyidmhoj/

17. "Analyse this: Jada Pinkett Smith." *The Jadafan.* Accessed August 30, 2009. http://jadapinkettsmith.blogspot.com/2007/04/analyse-this-jada-pinkett-smith.html.

18. Deggans, Eric. "Banking on Star Power." *St. Petersburg Times Online.* July 23, 2003. Accessed August 30, 2009. http://www.sptimes.com/2003/07/23/news_pf/Artsandentertainment/Banking_on_star_power.shtml

19. "Will Smith: Best Will in the world." *The Independent.* Accessed August 30, 2009. http://www.independent.co.uk/arts-entertainment/films/features/will-smith-best-will-in-the-world-552513.htm.

20. "9 Qs with Seven Pounds Star Will Smith." *Hollywood.com.* Accessed August 30, 2009. http://www.hollywood.com/feature/Interview_Seven_Pounds_Will_Smith/5368688.

21. "Smith sings at I, Robot premiere." *BBC NEWS*. Accessed August 30, 2009. http://news.bbc.co.uk/2/hi/entertainment/3537564.stm.

22. "Alex Proyas Will Answer Questions From /Film Readers." */Film | Blogging the Reel World*. Accessed August 30, 2009. http://www.slashfilm.com/2009/03/16/alex-proyas-will-answer-questions-from-film-readers/.

Will Smith, left, and his wife Jada Pinkett make an appearance at the Charlie Mack Party 1 Peace march Saturday, July 22, 2006, in Philadelphia. (AP Photo/H. Rumph Jr.)

Actor Will Smith arrives at the premiere of Lions for Lambs in Los Angeles in this, November 1, 2007, file photo. (AP Photo/Matt Sayles, file)

Actor Will Smith poses for a photo in Los Angeles in this November 30, 2007, file photo. The Anti-Defamation League said that it accepts Will Smith's explanation that he never praised Adolf Hitler in remarks the actor says were misinterpreted. (AP Photo/Kevork Djansezian, File)

Actor Will Smith, center, star of I Am Legend, holds the hands of his children Willow, left, and Jaden as he places his feet in cement during a hand and footprint ceremony at Grauman's Chinese Theater Monday, December 10, 2007, in the Hollywood section of Los Angeles. (AP Photo/Nick Ut)

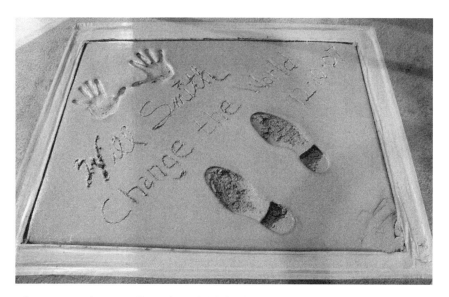

The imprints of actor Will Smith are left behind after he was honored with a hand and footprint ceremony at Grauman's Chinese Theater on December 10, 2007, in the Hollywood section of Los Angeles. (AP Photo/Nick Ut)

In this June 30, 2008, photo, from back row left, actor Will Smith, his son Trey Smith, wife Jada Pinkett-Smith, their son Jaden Smith, front left, and their daughter Willow Smith arrive at the Hancock premiere in Los Angeles. (AP Photo/Matt Sayles, file)

Actor Will Smith arrives at a screening of his new movie Seven Pounds, *in Valley View, Ohio, Thursday, November 20, 2008. (AP Photo/Jamie-Andrea Yanak)*

Chapter 6

ALCHEMY

The power of positive thinking: If we think it, dream it, it's a physical thrust toward our dreams.

—*Will Smith*

U.S. presidents George Washington, Abraham Lincoln, and Harry Truman never attended college, yet became extremely successful men. Although Will never attended college either, he was an articulate young man with a passion to learn. He once said that getting him to read anything in school was difficult, but he became an avid reader as he got older. One book that he said changed his life was *The Alchemist: A Fable About Following Your Dream,* which is an allegorical novel by Paulo Coelho, published in 1988. It is a story about Santiago, a young Spanish shepherd, on a journey to fulfill his personal legend.

This personal legend is the destined path that each one of us should take to achieve our greatest happiness. In the story, Santiago must go through various ups and downs in his experiences, all so that one day he will discover his personal legend. The book sold more than 65 million copies in more than 150 countries, becoming one of the best-selling books in history.

In various interviews, Will has talked honestly about the fact that he considered himself an alchemist looking for his own personal legend. To him, an alchemist is someone who follows his dreams and believes he can create whatever he wants to create. Will said, "If I can put my head on it right, study it, learn the patterns, and—it's hard to put into words, it's real metaphysical, esoteric nonsense, but I feel very strongly that we are who we choose to be."[1]

Early on in his career, Will said that he had chosen to become the biggest movie star in the world, and he was quickly heading in that direction. He firmly believed that his hard work, and what he calls his "sick work ethic" have combined with the principles of *The Alchemist* to push him even further. Some of those principles of *The Alchemist* are favorability, or beginner's luck, and the soul of the world. Will has said he believes in these principles so much that he has been teaching his children the principles of *The Alchemist* as well.

ROMANTIC LEADING MAN

The following year, Will decided to step away from action-packed blockbusters to do something he had yet to do in any of his movies—become the romantic leading man. In *Hitch,* which was released on February 2005, Will plays Alex "Hitch" Hitchens, a professional matchmaker who teaches men how to get a date with the woman they are interested in. Director Andy Tennant was thrilled to work with someone of Will's caliber.

"Part of the reason I wanted to do *Hitch* was because my other films had female protagonists. I wanted to do something with a male protagonist. To have a guy of his stature is a whole different ballgame," said Tennant. "It was like a good time around a pool table. With female stars, it was more like a nice candle-lit dinner. With Will, there were lots of laughs."[2]

The movie also stars Cuban actress Eva Mendes and comedian Kevin James. It is said that director Andy Tennant offered famed Bollywood actress Aishwarya Rai a part in the film, but she had to turn it down because she was working on a different film. Will has made it clear since then that he wants to work with Rai one day in another film. Casting for *Hitch's* female lead stirred up a little bit of controversy. Will explained that Eva Mendes was given the role opposite him because the producers were concerned that a black couple or a white actress would put viewers off.

Hollywood continued to expect big things from Will and watched as he released one successful movie after another, but now they might have been looking at him in a different light. He was an A-list, African American actor who had received an Oscar nomination and was one of Hollywood's leading men. The industry had come a long way in rewarding black actors with lead roles in movies, but even during the past few decades, lead roles for black actors were few and far between.

A CNN article on how blacks have fared in receiving Oscars and Oscar nominations cited a 2006 report by Russell Robinson, a professor of law at the University of California, Los Angeles, which exposes race-based casting in Hollywood. Robinson agreed that Will had been successful in overcoming racial boundaries because he's been profitable but also said that with Will's successes should come responsibility. As the biggest box-office star in the world, Robinson contends that Smith is obligated to push Hollywood to make changes for other African American actors. He uses Will's movie *Hitch* as an example.

"With Smith's 2005 film *Hitch*, the studio would not cast a black woman as Will Smith's love interest in the film because they didn't want the film to be a 'black film,'" Robinson said. "I would hope that Will challenged that decision. . . . I would hope that Will would try to get black actors hired."[3]

It is not known what Will did behind closed doors to push for a black actress. Tariq Mohammad, editor of BlackVoices.com, explains that sometimes actors of color get pigeonholed into roles, but Will has shown range, and hopefully this will open doors for other black actors and actresses. "The game in Hollywood is pleasing your fan base," said Mohammad. "He chooses the movies that are right for him. I think he turned down a role in *The Matrix*, and who knows if it would've been the same blockbuster if he had chosen it. I watched *Wild, Wild West* which had good chemistry and was funny enough to watch, but at the end of the day do you want that critical claim or will you settle for that blockbuster success."[4]

Hopefully, Will has the ability to open doors for other African American actors in the future, but when it comes to color in Hollywood, Will may be seen as green and not as black. "Hollywood sees green as in dollars, and that's just the bottom line. You have to show them you can make money with your story no matter what color the characters are," Mohammad said.[5] Will has said that movie stars are not made in America. "Movie stars are made when you can pull $20 million out of Brazil, or when you can do $48 million in Japan," he said.[6]

In his movie *Hitch,* Will's character falls in love with Sara Melas (played by Mendes), a gossip columnist who doesn't realize at first that Hitch is the date doctor who helped a client of his have a one-night stand with her best friend. Hitch is hired by Albert Brennaman, played by Kevin James, to help him get a date with the movie's celebrity, Allegra Cole (played by Amber Valletta). Sara tries to uncover who the date doctor really is, and throughout the movie, the secrets Hitch teaches to Albert don't work in Hitch's relationship with Sara. Once Sara finds out who Hitch really is, the two break up since Sara thinks that all she is getting are preplanned lines and no real emotional honesty. The rest of the movie focuses on what Hitch realizes about relationships and whether the couples come together.

The movie had a $70 million production budget but made more than $368 million worldwide. It broke Sony's record for best opening weekend for a romantic-comedy film. Rory Bruer, Sony's head of distribution at the time, said, "Will Smith certainly delivers, doesn't he? He's one of those rare stars that just appeals to everyone, men, women and children. There's no doubt he's somewhat of a king of action, but he is every bit as good in comedy."[7]

LIKE FATHER, LIKE SON

You can tell by looking at Will's choices of movies and his albums that he doesn't like to be predictable. He mixed things up a bit—from roles in action-packed movies such as *Independence Day* to more dramatic parts such as portraying Muhammad Ali in the film *Ali.* After being successful as a romantic leading man in *Hitch,* Will chose to change things up again in his next role, which he found one night while watching television.

Back in 1982, while young Will was attending high school and writing rap lyrics, Chris Gardner, a man living in San Francisco, was dealing with the type of hardship that Will would never see in his lifetime. Gardner, who had become a top trainee at the stock brokerage house Dean Witter Reynolds, was experiencing marital problems. Although achieving a position in the training program was a huge success, its low monthly stipend didn't allow Gardner to make ends meet. Then, his girlfriend ran off with their son. When she returned and gave Gardner custody, he found out that the place where he was staying didn't allow children, so he and his son were kicked out. They were left homeless.

Gardner moved from place to place with his son—sleeping at such places as homeless shelters, parks, and even a locked bathroom in a local train station. Eventually, Gardner asked for help at the Glide Memorial United Methodist Church for homeless women, and because of his son, Chris Jr., they obliged. Gardner went on to pass his licensing examination and become a full-time employee at Dean Witter Reynolds. In 1987, he left the firm to start his own company, Gardner Rich & Co., in Chicago, Illinois. He sold the company several years later in a multimillion-dollar deal and became CEO and founder of Christopher Gardner International Holdings, with offices in New York, Chicago, and San Francisco.

Gardner's rags-to-riches story is what Hollywood movies are made of, and that's exactly what drew Will to Gardner's story when he saw it one night on *20/20*. He chose to pursue the rights to the story and turn it into a major motion picture, entitled *The Pursuit of Happyness*. It is said that the spelling of *happyness* reflects the name of Chris Jr.'s daycare center.

"The story has elements that were almost counterintuitive" said Will. "We all do our own racial-profiling and the Black man fighting to have his son, or fighting to raise his son, fighting to be a father to his son is not the stereotypical picture that lives in our minds." Will said Gardner's story was "real and authentic" and "it felt like a story that I not only wanted to tell, but it felt like a story I needed to tell."[8]

Bruer knew that Will was perfect to play the part of Chris Gardner. "Audiences around the world love him (Will)," said Bruer, whose past hits with Will included *Men in Black* and *Hitch*. "Everyone who sees Will Smith or meets Will Smith feels like he could be their best friend. He has that type of charisma that resonates throughout whatever room he's in."[9]

However, although Will had the ability to draw audiences into a film emotionally and achieve financial success for Hollywood studios, Gardner still wasn't convinced that Will was the right actor to portray him. It wasn't until Gardner's daughter told him, "Dad, if he can play Muhammad Ali, he can play you" that he was finally convinced.[10] Gardner and Will signed a $10 million contract for the movie, which once again included an additional earning of 20 percent gross. Gardner came on board as a consultant, and Will hired the reverend from the Glide Memorial United Methodist Church to play himself in the movie to make it more realistic.

Once again joining Will in the movie was his real-life son Jaden, cast to play Gardner's son, Chris Jr. Although Gardner's real-life son was only a toddler when these incidents took place, adjustments were made for the movie. The movie reflects the love of a father and a son, and Will could definitely understand that.

Will was also a proud father when his younger son, Jaden, who was only eight years old at the time, earned this first feature film role. Actually, Jaden had only acted previously in his parent's UPN sitcom, *All of Us,* so he was new to the movie business. Will, the doting father, admitted that Jaden was a natural in front of the camera, but once joked, "If he wasn't my child, I'd have had to sabotage his performance! He was stealing way too many of my scenes."[11]

Like his role in *Ali,* Will also wanted his portrayal of Gardner to be as realistic as possible, so he immersed himself in the role. He wanted to *be* Chris Gardner, and this was the prime opportunity to use what his acting coach, Aaron Speiser, had taught him earlier about acting—finding the emotional pain of the character and digging deep to feel what he was acting. Will studied Gardner in a very in-depth way, the way he once studied Muhammad Ali. "I had never been studied before. But I've got to tell you . . . Will Smith played Chris Gardner better than Chris Gardner ever did," said Gardner.[12]

During his preparation one night, Will even took a walk with Gardner back to the place where it all happened. They walked where Gardner was once homeless and scared, wondering what was going to happen to him and his son. Will walked the same San Francisco streets with Gardner that he had once walked in the middle of the night. Will was trying to get into his emotions and feel what Gardner was feeling on those dreadful nights.

"One night I took this cat on a walk through San Francisco. Biggest movie star in the world with no security, nothing. It's midnight," said Gardner. "We go to some of the places my son and I had to sleep. The park. Subway stations. We get to the public bathroom. It's a place I don't need to be. So I walked out. Will stayed inside. Seven minutes. I timed it. When he came out, he wasn't Will Smith anymore. He was Chris Gardner. A transformation took place. That's what you see on the screen."[13]

Director Gabriele Muccino also worked with Will to help pull more emotion out of him. Will explained how he was pushed by Muccino to not pose for the camera and said that Muccino insisted he would shut down the set until Will found the hurt and the feelings he needed to feel. Muccino even told Will he recognized one particular face that Will used with red eyes. It was the same face, Muccino said, that he used at end of *Men in Black*, so Muccino asked Will to change his facial expressions.

Interestingly, one of the most famous lines in *The Pursuit of Happyness* comes when Gardner is talking to his son and inadvertently hurts the child's feelings. To help repair the damage, Gardner says to Chris Jr., "Don't ever let anyone tell you that you can't do something—even me." That one prophetic line can probably be used to sum up Will's philosophy on his own life and his own acting abilities.

Will, like Gardner, has set out to do whatever he wants to do in his career. Taking on the role of Chris Gardner in *The Pursuit of Happyness* was no exception. At this point in his career, Will had 16 years of acting experience under his belt, and it was obvious that he had grown as an actor—from entering the industry as a young rapper and achieving television stardom as a teen on *The Fresh Prince of Bel-Air* to becoming the star of action-packed blockbuster movies to portraying the greatest boxer of all time, a cowboy, a romantic lead, and now Chris Gardner in a film that's an emotional tearjerker.

Away from the cameras, in Will's personal life, he was a grown man and father of three. He couldn't relate to Gardner's homeless situation at all. After all, compared to Gardner's tumultuous life, Will had it good. He had hardworking parents who loved him. He has had a good life, even with a divorce and losing millions along the way. On the other hand, Gardner had seen it all since he was a young boy—foster homes, abuse, fighting, and homelessness. But Will and Gardner had one common bond—the love of their sons. They were both fathers, and this was such a deep bond. The fact that Will was acting with his real-life son Jaden helped him to bring depth and emotion to the role and to one powerfully emotional scene in particular.

In the scene, Gardner is searching for a place for to stay for the night. With nowhere else to go, he ends up taking his son into an empty subway bathroom, where he locks the door, and his son falls asleep on his lap for the night. When someone tries to enter the bathroom, a frightened Gardner holds it closed with his foot while trying not to wake his sleeping son. Gardner quietly sobs himself to sleep.

Mick LaSalle, a writer for the *San Francisco Chronicle*, wondered where Will found the intense emotion for that, and other, scenes:

> Will Smith has the right quality for the role—he's an easy man to root for—but he augments this by channeling some inner quality of desperation and need. Frankly, I don't know where he found it; Smith was touched by luck at a very young age. Yet he does find it. In the taxicab scene, in which he tries to impress a prospective employer by solving the Rubik's Cube, and in every other scene in which Chris has to sit or stand there smiling while another man pronounces on his fate, Smith is right there with the right emotions: absolute hope and total terror.[14]

Will explains that it was easy to find the emotion for the bathroom scene when your own son is sitting in your lap. "I was in my scene with my actual son in my lap and it's that feeling of ultimate parental failure," said Will. "No acting necessary. My feelings were just there."[15]

The Pursuit of Happyness was a feel-good Christmas movie, released on December 15, 2006. It debuted in the number one spot at the box office, earning more than $27 million. *The Pursuit of Happyness* became Will's sixth consecutive number one opening. Overall, the film grossed more than $304 million worldwide. Once again, Hollywood stood up and took notice of Will's dramatic acting, just as they had in response to *Ali*. *Rolling Stone's* movie reviewer, Gabriele Muccino wrote, "Smith wins our hearts without losing his dignity, as Chris suits up for success by day and fights off despair by night. The role needs gravity, smarts, charm, humor and a soul that's not synthetic. Smith brings it. He's the real deal."[16]

Will is so much the real deal that in one scene, Gardner solves the challenging Rubik's cube puzzle in under a minute to impress his potential employer, who didn't think it could be done. To do this scene right, Will wanted to really learn how to do the same thing, so that it would look realistic in the movie, so he found someone to teach him. Once he learned how to do it, he solved the puzzle live on a talk show, again in under a minute, to prove to the audience that he really could do it. You could even hear Will panting and talking his way through it until it was completed!

ACADEMY AWARD, AGAIN

On February 25, 2007, almost five years to the day that Will was nominated for his first Academy Award, he was once again sitting in the Kodak Theater in Los Angeles, waiting to find out if he had won the award for Best Actor in a Leading Role. His wife, Jada, and his youngest son, Jaden, sat with him. This time, his competition was Leonardo DiCaprio for his role as Danny Archer in *Blood Diamond*, Ryan Gosling for his role as Dan Dunne in *Half Nelson*, Peter O'Toole for his role as Maurice in *Venus*, and Forest Whitaker for his role as Idi Amin in *The Last King of Scotland*.

This time, it was Forest Whitaker who would walk away with the coveted Oscar. But Will and Jaden wouldn't be empty handed for their work. They each received several other nominations and awards for their work, including Golden Globe nominations for best actor, and Black Reel awards for Best Actor (Will) and Best Breakthrough Performer (Jaden). The duo was also nominated for NAACP Image Awards for both outstanding actor and supporting actor in a motion picture, and the movie won the NAACP Image Award for Outstanding Motion Picture. Jaden also won the MTV Movie Award for Best Male Breakthrough Performance.

Although Will understood that box-office receipts and awards were important to Hollywood, he didn't judge his own success by those standards this time around. Instead, he judged his success in portraying Chris

Gardner by the reaction of the subject himself, Chris Gardner. It's the same way that Will judged his portrayal of *Ali*. Will knew that Muhammad Ali and Chris Gardner needed to love their movies, no matter how much money the films made or how many awards Will or the movies received.

"If Chris doesn't like it, it's a failure," said Will. "He turned around after the film. I'm sitting there and my heart is jumping and he looked and he said, 'I can't even talk to you right now.' He got up and walked out. I was like, 'Well, what the hell does that mean?' But then we really went outside and he was crying. He just thanked me for the service to his family and he's forever indebted for bringing his story [to the big screen]. And for me, it was a win from that point, so all of this is gravy time now."[17]

Will's portrayal of Chris wasn't the only thing that Hollywood noticed in *The Pursuit of Happyness*. Hollywood saw that Jaden was a good young actor, and other opportunities started to come up for him. Jaden's next role was with actor Keanu Reeves in *The Day the Earth Stood Still*, which would be released in 2008. It was a remake of the 1951 movie of the same name, and Jaden played Jacob Bensen, the eight-year-old stepson of Helen Benson, played by Jennifer Connolly. Connolly said that working with the young actor was fantastic and she said Jaden had a lot to offer, doing his job beautifully.[18]

It's already been said that Will and Jada have encouraged their children to follow their dreams, but they haven't specifically encouraged them to become actors or singers. However, they haven't discouraged their children from following in their footsteps either. It was all about what made them happy. So if Jaden wanted to act, it was okay with them.

Will still maintains a very close relationship with his first-born son, Trey, who resides with Will's ex-wife, Sheree. Sheree is now remarried to former San Diego Charger Terrell Fletcher, and together they have a daughter named Jodie. Trey had some acting jobs when he was younger—he served as *Access Hollywood's* special correspondent for events such as Nickelodeon's *Kids Choice Awards* and also guest-starred in the UPN sitcom *All of Us*. But at this point, Trey is a 16-year-old high school student who doesn't necessarily have a desire to have an acting career. He's a tall, good-looking boy who attends Oaks Christian High School in Westlake Village, California, and he is a wide-receiver for their football team. For now, Trey prefers to play football rather than act.

"I know this," said Steve Clarkson, a quarterback guru, who trained Trey. "He loves playing wide-receiver. But it's something he does naturally, that he doesn't necessarily have to work at. If he ever decided that this is what he wanted to do, I truly believe he'd have the ability to someday be a first-round pick. No question."[19]

Although Will was deep into his rap career by the time he was Trey's age, Will understands that Trey needs—and has plenty of—time to decide on his career choice. However, Will's younger children, Jaden and Willow, were already showing signs that they would follow in mom and dad's footsteps. After watching her big brother hit the big screen, seven-year-old Willow caught the acting bug as well. She auditioned—which was a huge requirement from her parents—for and earned her first role in Will's next feature film, *I Am Legend*. Will once compared his kids to Johnny Depp and Paris Hilton. He explained how Jaden was like Johnny Depp and just wanted to make good movies, while Willow was more like Paris Hilton and just wanted to be on television.[20]

In December 2007, Will's next movie, *I Am Legend*, which was based on the 1954 sci-fi/horror novel of the same name written by Richard Matheson, hit the theaters. New York City is the setting of the movie *I Am Legend*, although the novel is set in Los Angeles. *I Am Legend* was set in the near future—the years 2009 and 2012 to be exact. Will played Robert Neville, a scientist who can't stop an incurable man-made virus from killing every human on earth. Neville is immune to the virus and is the last known human survivor. He searches to find other survivors, but instead of human survivors, he finds mutant victims. His mission is to find a way to reverse the virus by using the only thing he thinks might work—his own immune blood—but time is of the essence.

Matheson's popular novel was made into a major motion picture on two other occasions. The first was *The Last Man on Earth* in 1964, which starred Vincent Price, and the second was *The Omega Man* in 1971, which starred the veteran actor Charleston Heston.

As is typical in Hollywood, *I Am Legend* had a few production stops and starts before filming even started. Warner Bros., which owned the rights to the book, had major budgeting issues and had to shelve the project for quite awhile. They tried to ramp up production again in 2002, but it wasn't until 2005 that Warner Bros. approached Will and asked him if he wanted to work with writer Akiva Goldsman, who had worked with Will before on *I, Robot*. Will agreed to do the film.

Once again, Will had a unique way of preparing himself for a different role. In order to prepare for his role as Neville, Will traveled to Atlanta, Georgia, where he visited the Centers for Disease Control (CDC). The CDC is a federal agency in the Department of Health and Human Services that investigates, diagnoses, and tries to control or prevent diseases. It was a great place for Will to learn what he needed to for his role in *I Am Legend*.

In addition, he left Jada and the kids at home while he immersed himself in virtual isolation in New York City to thoroughly understand what might be going through his character's head when he is alone for days and days at a time.

"I just said I needed five, six days by myself," he said. "I wanted to know what's going to happen inside my head if I just confine myself and it's just bizarre what happens when you are forced to be alone. It's really like a dangerous psychological place, to not have contact with other people. You know, we've all sat on the freeway and wished everybody else was dead, but you really desperately need even uncomfortable contact with other people. It's almost like good bacteria."[21]

In addition to flying solo for a few days, he and the producers looked at other types of people who have been subjected to periods of intense isolation. They studied prisoners of war and other prisoners and discovered the importance of a routine to these people. "The only way to maintain sanity is that you had to have a regimented schedule. That was the basis of how we tried to create my character in the movie, and then also the idea of his internal monologue. When you have no external stimulus, you lose the stimulus-response concept with your thoughts and feelings. A guy told us you that you forget the names of simple things, when you no longer have the stimulus and response," said Will.[22]

Will's *I Am Legend* performance was compared to that of Tom Hanks's performance in his Academy Award–winning role in the 2000 movie *Cast Away*. In the movie, Tom plays a Federal Express employee whose plane crashes on a deserted island. For more than an hour of the movie, which equates to about three years of the character's life, Hanks doesn't speak. In the same vein, Will has a lengthy period in *I Am Legend* where he depends only on his body and facial language to communicate to the audience, and his only costar is his dog, Samantha. *Variety* magazine said of Will's performance, "Smith manages it very well, showboating only briefly to show off his newly trim physique and intermittently displaying the incipient madness that would surely come from being alone against an unrelenting threat."[23]

Although *I Am Legend* is considered an action-packed special-effects movie, it wasn't released during July, the typical time of year that Will owns the box office. Instead, it was released at Christmas time, an unusual move considering Will's past success with movies of this kind being summer blockbusters. Perhaps it was a leap of faith, but Will had studied the industry closely and knew what made a movie successful.

Years ago, Will remembers, when he said "I want to be the biggest movie star in the world," he and his agent sat down and reviewed what kinds of movies were the most successful in Hollywood. Will and his agent discovered that all of the top 10 greatest movies lists included special-effects movies. Nine out of 10 of those movies had creatures in them. Eight out of 10 of those movies had creatures and a love story. When Will was making the decision to sign onto *Independence Day*, he realized that the film met these criteria. Based on that, Will found the decision to make *I Am Legend* an easy one.[24] As a matter of fact, it didn't matter when they released the movie, it had the makings to be a hit anytime it was released.

Just a few days before the opening of *I Am Legend*, Will did something else that would further, and literally, cement his legendary status in Hollywood. By 2007 Will had already left his imprint in Hollywood's record books, so it was only fitting that Graumann's Chinese Theater invited Will to leave his actual hand prints directly on Hollywood Boulevard. This is a time-honored Hollywood tradition, and only a few select celebrities have been invited to join the exclusive society known as the Forecourt to the Stars.

Anyone, including fans, can nominate a celebrity as long as the celebrity and their management is in agreement with the nomination. There are more than 200 nominations per year. Once all of the nominations have come in, a committee reviews the nominations and renders a final decision. Each year, approximately 20 celebrities are selected for this honor.

When a celebrity is asked to become part of this legendary tradition, he or she joins other Hollywood celebrities who have been asked to do the same. These legends include actress Marilyn Monroe, actor John

Wayne, actor and singer Jimmy Durante, actor Tom Hanks, actress Betty Grable, the young Harry Potter actors, comedian and actor Bob Hope, and more. During Will's ceremony, he wrote the words "Change the World" next to his hand prints. Will's friend, fellow actor Tom Cruise, joined him at this legendary event as well as at the red-carpet opening of *I Am Legend*.

CRUISIN' ALONG

Normally, a friendship between A-list movie stars wouldn't spark any questions, concerns, or tabloid controversy, but Will's friendship with actor Tom Cruise has done just that. Tom Cruise was already a popular actor who had a long and successful movie career. He is well-known for such movie blockbusters as *Top Gun* (1986), *The Color of Money* (1986), *Rain Man* (1988), *Born on the Fourth of July* (1989), and *Jerry McGuire* (1996). He also became one of the top Hollywood wage earners, commanding a $15 million salary for every movie because, like Will, his movies were successful at the box office. Cruise went on to receive Academy Award nominations for *Born on the Fourth of July*, *Jerry McGuire*, and *Magnolia*. He won several Golden Globe Awards, and in 2006 *Forbes* magazine named him the most powerful celebrity of the year, only one year before he showed up at the opening of Will's film and the celebration at Graumann's Chinese Theater.

Tom was one of the most popular actors in Hollywood. He was once married to actress Mimi Rogers, whom he later divorced, and then he married actress Nicole Kidman. He and Kidman adopted two children, but the marriage also ended in divorce. In May 2005, Tom Cruise made a notable appearance on *The Oprah Winfrey Show*. During what has since been called the couch incident, Cruise confessed his love for actress Katie Holmes by jumping on Oprah's couch and falling to his knees. The incident shocked fans and caused them to question his stability. Cruise's solid Hollywood reputation was tarnished for some time after that incident, and he became fodder for tabloids and comedians.

To add fuel to the fire, a few weeks later Cruise appeared on *The Today Show* where he and host Matt Lauer got into a debate about Cruise's denouncement of prescription medication for psychiatric conditions and Cruise's negative comments about actress Brooke Shields, who had used medication to help her battle postpartum depression.

Cruise once claimed that it was his religion, Scientology, that cured him of his dyslexia (a learning disability mostly with written language, especially reading), and that Scientologists didn't believe in using anti-depressants. There are other celebrities who have, at one time, admitted that they are also members of the Church of Scientology, including John Travolta and his wife Kelly Preston, Lisa Marie and Priscilla Presley, and Kirstie Alley. There has been an ongoing debate as to whether Scientology is a cult or a religion.

According to its own written history, Scientology was founded by L. Ron Hubbard and "follows a long tradition of religious practice. Its roots lie in the deepest beliefs and aspirations of all great religions, thus encompassing a religious heritage as old and as varied as man himself. Though drawing upon the wisdom of some 50,000 years, Scientology is a new religion, one which has isolated fundamental laws of life and, for the first time, developed a workable technology that can be applied to help one achieve a happier and more spiritual existence. Scientology is therefore something one does, not merely something one believes in."[25]

After both of Cruise's talk show appearances, and his appearances at Will's events, fans and tabloids began to wonder if the *Mission Impossible* actor was spending time with Will simply to convert him to Scientology. It became a topic of conversation in the media for the next few years as reporters tried to find out what Cruise's intentions were. Interestingly, Will admitted to the media that Cruise introduced him and Jada to the study of Scientology: "I was introduced to it by Tom, and I'm a student of world religion. I was raised in a Baptist household. I went to a Catholic school, but the ideas of the Bible are 98% the same ideas of Scientology, 98% the same ideas of Hinduism and Buddhism."[26]

Although Will and Jada share many aspects of their personal lives with fans and the media, they weren't the type of Hollywood couple that spoke openly about their religion or various other private aspects of their lives. Certain things were just off limits. However, they have at times adamantly denied that they are Scientologists. Will has even said that his grandmother would roll over in her grave if he became one. Over the next few years, however, the couple would be questioned even more about their true religious beliefs, especially after making several questionable donations.

While the media was trying to figure out Cruise's true motives for befriending the megastar, Will had another blockbuster movie to promote.

I Am Legend opened to an extremely successful $77 million weekend and earned a whopping total of $585 million. *I Am Legend* became Will's 11th number one movie opening and the 7th in a row. *I Am Legend* also became the best December movie opening in Hollywood history, ousting *The Lord of the Rings: The Return of the King* in 2003.[27]

Tom Cruise and Katie Holmes gave birth to their daughter, Suri Cruise, on April 18, 2006, and married later that year, on November 19, 2006. It's common for celebrities to show off their babies in magazines or to release a photo of the baby to the tabloids, but when Cruise and Holmes didn't do that, more questions surfaced about whether the baby even existed. Some questioned the practices of Scientology, guessing that the religion required the couple to keep the baby hidden, while others just said the couple wanted privacy.

Once again, because of their friendship with the couple, Jada and Will were caught in the middle of a Tom Cruise and Scientology controversy. Jada stood by her friends' side and spoke up on behalf of the couple, confirming the existence of the baby and sharing that Suri was beautiful. Again, the couple's connection to Cruise and Holmes, and their connection to Scientology, came into question. It wouldn't be the last time.

After attending wedding ceremony for Cruise and Holmes, Will and Jada decided to renew their own wedding vows. Will said, "We just came back from Tom and Katie's wedding. So, that made me realize we didn't have a big wedding. They had a real wedding. It was just the most amazing, beautiful, wonderful, fairytale experience ever and I was just sitting beside Jada going, 'Phew!' I hadn't had too much success when we got married, so I couldn't afford that. Ten years—we're going to go back and do it again—renew the vows and all that."[28]

Even though Will was busy talking to the media about *I Am Legend*, he was already filming another movie. It had almost become a routine for Will to promote and film at the same time—it was almost superhuman. And in his next movie, he would actually play a superhero, but not the kind that audiences loved, like Batman, Superman, or Spiderman. Instead, Will would once again step out of the box and do something different for his next role.

Will would portray John Hancock, a jerk of a superhero who had a serious drinking problem. To prepare for this role, Will watched other movie and television characters that he called "obnoxious jerks," including the comedian W. C. Fields and *All in the Family's* Archie Bunker. "W.C. Fields was hilarious by being mean to kids. And Archie Bunker was a jerk, but he was hilarious," he said.[29]

Hancock was yet another movie that had gone through the ups and downs of Hollywood predevelopment. It was originally written in 1996 by screenwriter Vincent Ngo, and then rewritten by two new writers, Vince Gilligan and John August. The movie then bounced through various directors until the final director, Peter Berg, finished the film. Even the title of the movie changed several times—starting out as *Tonight He Comes*, then changing to *John Hancock* and finally just *Hancock*. The film also went through several changes in the ratings as well, initially receiving an R rating by the Motion Picture Association of America (MPAA).

According to the MPAA, the movie ratings system is a voluntary system operated by the MPAA and the National Association of Theater Owners (NATO). The ratings are given by a board of parents who comprise the Classification and Rating Administration (CARA). CARA's board members view each film and, after a group discussion, vote on its rating. The ratings are intended to provide parents with advance information so they can decide for themselves which films are appropriate for viewing by their own children. The board uses the same criteria as any parent making a judgment—theme, language, violence, nudity, sex, and drug use are among content areas considered in the decision-making process. Once the directors removed questionable scenes and various vulgarities, the movie received a more suitable PG-13 rating.

The production budget for *Hancock* was huge—topping $150 million—and then there was Will's $20 million salary plus 20 percent of gross. This time, Will's contract also included a *pay-or-play* clause, which assured that he would get paid even if the movie wasn't filmed or finished. Contract stipulations like this are common in the industry and protect the actor's investment of time in a movie, since they cannot work on any other movie while filming the one they are contracted to complete.

Will wasn't too worried about how this particular box-office opening would go, because he knew it would be successful. However, there was someone at home who was worried. Seven-year-old Willow, fresh off her role in her dad's movie *I Am Legend*, had earned another feature

film role in *Kit Kittredge: An American Girl,* a comedy-drama directed by
Patricia Rozema. The movie focused on the American Girl character Kit
Kittredge, who lives in Cincinnati, Ohio, during the Great Depression.
The film was the first American Girl film to have a theatrical release,
but it released on July 2, 2008, in direct competition with Will's movie
Hancock.

When it came to her acting career, Willow exuded the same confidence that her parents have. She even boasted during an interview that
she was going to beat her dad at the box office. Will joked back saying,
"'Sorry baby, but I got to stomp on you." Unfortunately, little curly haired
Willow would have to wait until she was in a different movie to beat her
dad at the box office.

Although *American Girl* did well and grossed $17 million overall, it
only grossed $3 million during its opening weekend. Will, however, re-
turned to his Fourth of July success. It was *Hancock* that stole the number one spot at the box office that weekend. By the end of the weekend,
Will had another number one hit on his record, and *Hancock* had earned
more than $107 million. It became the third-biggest Fourth of July week-
end opening ever after the movies *Transformers* and *Spider-Man 2.* It was
also Will's fifth film to open on a Fourth of July weekend and was his
most successful opening to date. If breaking these records wasn't enough,
the film was also Will's 8th film in a row to take the top spot and the
12th film in his career to lead the box office.

At the *Hancock* movie premiere, Will surprised those who attended
and returned to his rap roots, reuniting with his pal and long-time partner DJ Jazzy Jeff. The duo performed for those who showed up at the
premiere and sang their classic song, "Summertime." Will and Jazz were
still popular; when they tried to leave, the fans started chanting, asking
the pair to perform "Brand New Funk."[30]

Although it was marketed as a comedy, *Hancock* wasn't a movie where
the audience was going to love Will's character. The character Hancock
was meant to be lonely and loathed, not loved. As popular as the movie
was at the box office, *Hancock* didn't quite get the laughs and attention
that the studios had hoped for, and it didn't receive the best reviews.
Some movie critics said that the first part of the film was good but that
the second half fell apart. One reviewer said that in the last hour of the
movie, "The zaniness evaporates, leaving behind a last half-hour that's

sour and sentimental at the same time, not to mention overloaded with weird, illogical developments."[31] In its second week at the box office, *Hancock* dropped in gross ticket sales. Nevertheless, Will was still very popular with his audiences, especially the kids, as the movie won Best Summer Action/Adventure Movie at the 2008 Teen Choice Awards.

It still seemed that the Golden Boy could do no wrong. Even the Will Smith movies that critics panned still earned respectable amounts of money for Hollywood. The industry never seemed afraid to put out a movie as long as it starred Will Smith, and it almost seemed that anything the Philly native wanted to show Hollywood that he could do, they would agree to. Veteran movie critic Leonard Maltin once said of Will, "Like other smart actors, he used his successful films as a bargaining chip to make riskier movies. He's telling his audience now, 'you like me. Now please trust me to take you in a different direction. I won't steer you wrong.'"[32]

This career almost seemed too easy, too cushy for Will. But, believe it or not, there was a time in his life when Will got scared about releasing a movie. He had taken risks before—for example, with *Wild, Wild West, Ali,* and *The Pursuit of Happyness*—but releasing his next movie really scared him. Will actually wondered if this next movie would succeed with audiences who only liked and expected high-budget blockbusters from him. "It's terrifying because the end of the movie is huge in American cinemas—how you send them out of the theater is how people are going to react to your movie, so there's always the big action sequence and the wild music with the strings and you clap," he said.[33]

The movie that he was scared of was called *Seven Pounds*. It didn't have the big action sequences that his other movies had, nor did it have wild rap music or the nicely packaged happy ending that left the audiences clapping. The movie didn't pass Will's successful formula criteria that he and his agent decided years ago would make him the biggest star in the world. Instead, Will's next movie had a somber ending—one that would send the audiences into a tailspin and leave the theater questioning what had just happened. However, Will saw *Seven Pounds* as a totally new journey for him—a place he's been scared of traveling to before. He has said that this movie allowed him to deliver on ideas and concepts that are powerful and meaningful to him and to audiences, but it was a new skill for him to be able to do that.[34]

Looking back, Will's last few movies were progressively more darker than his earlier ones. There was the homeless single dad, the alcoholic superhero, and a man who faced an illness that wiped out a population and left him alone—but the story line of *Seven Pounds* focuses solely on death. There would be no explosions and no aliens. It would be a story simply about death, and that's exactly what Will wanted it to be.

> I [wanted to] explore the concept of death, both literal and figurative. A divorce is a death of sorts, the death of a dream. Losing your job is a death. Losing a loved one. I got intrigued by the idea of how . . . human beings manage trauma. Why would the only certainty in life be the most difficult thing to deal with? Part of the pain, at least in the West, is our linear view: Something's born, it lives, and death is the end. Then I realized it's actually not how it works. You bend that straight line into a circle, and it's birth, life, death, rebirth. Being prepared for that rebirth is the sweet spot in storytelling for me.[35]

In *Seven Pounds*, Will plays Ben Thomas, an IRS agent who finds that his life circumstances have changed rather dramatically. In the movie, two years earlier, Ben Thomas caused a car crash where seven people died—six strangers and his fiancée. As a result, Ben decided to donate seven parts of his body to seven people before he decides to end his own life. He donates a lung lobe to his brother and part of his liver to a child, and he starts looking for others to donate to. On the way, he meets someone to donate a kidney to and someone to whom he can donate bone marrow. In effect, he decides to change the lives of seven other people whom he has handpicked. One person is Emily Posa (played by Rosario Dawson), a young woman who is suffering from a serious heart condition and who has a rare blood type as well.

Former *Cheers* actor and motion-picture star Woody Harrelson played Ezra Turner, a lonely blind man. Harrelson said that he really enjoyed working with Will for the first time: "I was so nervous about playing a blind piano player and Will came in and he was just patting people on the back and giving hugs and I thought, it's pretty amazing that the biggest star in the world is one of the nicest guys in the world."[36]

Seven Pounds was another opportunity for Will to use what his acting coach once taught him. Will had to look for something deep within him to connect to his character, so he chose the emotions he felt when his grandmother had died from a stroke a few years ago. "I never cried about it and always adopted the attitude that she was in a better place, that it was for the best because of the stroke and how ill she was. I'm sure I drew on that because it gave me permission to feel things that you don't normally or I don't normally like to show. I guess it's healing in that way," he said.[37]

In the movie, Ben donates parts of his body—his heart, a lung, part of his liver, his eyes, and more—to people that Ben deems worthy. As Ben gets to know these people and others, he reflects on his life, what decisions he has made in the past, and the meaning of everything he's done. The movie is directed by Gabriele Muccino, who directed Will in his other Oscar-nominated role, *The Pursuit of Happyness*.

Except for the movie *Hitch*, Will hadn't had many romantic lead roles, and since his wedding to Jada, getting through love scenes was a bit tougher for the veteran actor and long-time husband. In *Seven Pounds*, Will has a romantic scene with Rosario Dawson's character, Emily. Dawson also enjoyed working with Will: "He was amazing. The chemistry between these two characters was so important. We really fell in love with these characters . . . He was incredibly gracious and amazing throughout, up until that point when he was really resisting and fighting being this person."[38] However, Dawson revealed that Will wouldn't start his kissing scenes for weeks. "It would be on the schedule, we'd have lights and everything set up, and he would end up being like, 'I'm not feeling it tonight. I don't think it's going to happen. Let's wait another week,'" said Dawson. "I was checking my breath, smelling myself, trying to see: 'Am I offending the man in some way?'"[39]

Will finally filmed the kissing scenes, and the movie premiered the week before Christmas in 2008. It earned $167 million, not quite the blockbuster Will is used to, but the movie made more at the box office than was anticipated since it wasn't getting great reviews before it opened. Unfortunately, the film didn't receive great reviews after it opened either, with one reviewer, Brian Tallerico of Hollywood Chicago, calling *Seven Pounds* "one of Will's misfires that brings it crashing to the ground." He also said it's "a mess, a film of conflicting tones and arguably offensive themes, a movie that moves beyond traditional melodrama in just the first few minutes and keeps flying into the over-the-top stratosphere."

Seven Pounds definitely wasn't Will's best movie, but even when he's not as his best, he still manages to bring in decent box-office receipts. However, this might be enough evidence for Will and for Hollywood that even though audiences love Will, they prefer to see him in films where he is the good guy and the film has a happy ending.

CHARITABLE WILL

In 2008, Will turned 40 years old, and before celebrating this momentous occasion, he wrote a constitution for himself, inspired by our country's founding fathers, which said that he would make everyone he meets a better person. "Grandma was always smiling, I know why I'm here; I'm here to make everyone a better person," he said.[40]

Perhaps it was the fact that Will has already put more than two decades of experience into this entertainment industry or the fact that he was now a middle-aged father of three, or that he had the financial resources to be able to help others. Whatever the reason, Will knew that it was the time in his career to start giving back, and he started by going straight to the people. He had already participated in Live Aid, a worldwide string of benefit concerts that helped to raise money and awareness for poverty. On July 2, 2005, Will opened the concert in Philadelphia.

While he was promoting his latest movie, *Seven Pounds*, Will took the opportunity to do more charitable work. In the past, Will's movies were uniquely promoted and marketed using various creative techniques—whether it was the famed Super Bowl commercial for *Independence Day* or the suspenseful marketing of the movie *I Am Legend*, which included posters that teased viewers with the copy, "The last man on Earth . . . is not alone." However, *Seven Pounds* was promoted a little differently. Will actually boarded a tour bus and went directly to the people, something that is rarely done by a celebrity with such A-list status. The bus made stops across the country, but it wasn't just to meet reporters and other writers. Will wanted to take the time to meet his fans and, as he wrote on his cemented handprints at the Graumann's Chinese Theater, to "Change the World."

For example, one such stop on this bus tour was in Minneapolis, Minnesota, where Will stopped to visit students at local schools and patients at area hospitals. In Edina, Minnesota, the *Seven Pounds* premier turned into a fund-raiser for the Second Harvest Heartland, Minnesota's largest hunger-relief organization.[41] In St. Louis, Louisiana, Will visited St. Louis Children's Hospital as well as two area schools during his visit and credited his grandmother with teaching him how to try to make a difference in others' lives.[42] In Charlotte, North Carolina, Will helped to raise awareness for the Second Harvest Food Bank. He promoted the film and donated 300 turkeys to Second Harvest at a red carpet gala, which was open to the public.[43]

"It's given me a chance to talk to the people and see what they want and what they need," said Will. "I visited hospitals and other places just to reconnect and hope to do it more before the films. That's one way to stay in sync with my fans."[44] Will also made a surprise visit to a Lake Highlands High School pep rally in Dallas, Texas, to which he brought along Tony Romo, quarterback of the Dallas Cowboys.

In 2008, *Forbes* magazine named Will Hollywood's highest paid actor and stated that he was worth an estimated $80 million per year. This gave him the top spot on their annual Celebrity Top 100 best-paid actors list. "Will seems like a very genuine, thoughtful, likeable and kind person," said Tariq Mohammad, director of AOL's Black Voices. "He's been more successful than anyone and transitioned from an actor to a producer in Hollywood. I can't think of anyone who has done that. I applaud him and the hard work that he put in to do it. He wasn't always the million-dollar film person. He was a rapper who had a gift and had to work and hone that. The fruits of labor—work hard you can develop your gifts into from years to come."[45]

Because of Will and Jada's successes, they were also named one of Hollywood's power couples by *Forbes* magazine, joining the ranks of such other power couples as music moguls Beyonce and Jay-Z, who between them made $162 million in one year and took the number one spot. Will and Jada owned the second position. Other big names rounding out the list were David and Victoria Beckham (worth $58 million), Tim McGraw and Faith Hill (worth $35 million), and Brad Pitt and Angelina Jolie (worth $34 million). Other couples such as Will's friends Tom Cruise and Katie Holmes, Keith Urban and Nicole Kidman, and Ben Affleck and Jennifer Garner were also on the list.

Will had come a long way since the days when he spent his earnings on extravagant items and owed the IRS millions. Instead, he was a responsible adult and was ready to give back to the less fortunate. Jada had donated $1 million to her high school alma mater, the Baltimore School for the Arts, from which she graduated in 1989. She had asked that a theater there be dedicated to one of her classmates, rapper Tupac Shakur. The Baltimore School for the Arts announced the donation for a renovation and expansion and said it would name a new theater for her.

Although Will and Jada homeschooled their kids Jaden and Willow, the couple also decided to launch a new elementary school, the New Village Leadership Academy in their hometown of Calabasas, California. The couple had long dreamed of opening up a school of their own, where children could feel excited about learning. They founded The Leadership Academy, which was for prekindergarten through sixth-grade students. The school can currently accommodate 60 students, although Jada would eventually like to expand the school and open another center for high school students.

The decision to open a new school was exciting, especially since the school's celebrity founders had the financial resources to fund such a project. But this new school had tongues wagging because it once again fueled speculation about the couples' involvement with Scientology. Will and Jada had previously donated $122,500 to Scientology causes, and it was first rumored that the school would be based on Scientology principles.

It had been said that the Smiths would use a Hubbard-influenced teaching method called *study technology*. It was also said that the curriculum included academic skills as well as everyday living skills, such as etiquette, yoga, and technology. The school would also include a no-sugar policy and encourage parents to limit their children's television time. In addition, their Web site confirms that several teachers are also Scientologists.

The media jumped all over Will and Jada's decision to build the school, and the tabloids marked them as the new faces of Scientology, even though to date they have never come out and actually said that the curriculum is based on Scientology. However, the Web site for the school states the following though: "Parents are also welcome to take the Learning How to Learn course at the school and we encourage this as it demystifies what Study Technology is. Though developed by L. Ron Hubbard, it is a secular course and not affiliated with the religion of Scientology, just as the Montessori method, though developed by a devout Catholic, is not a way to teach religious concepts."[46]

Once again, Will and Jada had to answer to an outpouring of questions from the media surrounding their involvement with Scientology as well as their friendship with Tom Cruise. Defending his friend once again, Will said he was bothered by how the entertainment media handled Cruise's ties to Scientology and how Cruise reacted on *The Oprah Winfrey Show* and *The Today Show*. "That's painful for me to see. I've met very few people committed to goodness the way Tom is," said Will. "We disagree on a lot of things. . . . But even with different faiths and different beliefs, at the end of the day, goodness is goodness."[47]

When asked how he handled it all, Will said, "You have to let that roll off you. There's a natural narcotic my brain must pump, because negativity doesn't last. It's strange to play a guy like Hancock, who can't find something to feel good about. That's the opposite of who I am."[48]

Will's friendship with Cruise has a deeper meaning to Will since Cruise understands what it is like to be an A-list megastar in Hollywood. Cruise has also helped Will review his scripts. Each actor respects the other, but neither sees any competition in getting film roles. "Tom just broke it down to me and said, Will, we are not competing, so don't think that way. That blew my mind because that is not how this business works at all," Will said.[49]

Continuing their charitable work, Jada and Will have also founded the Will and Jada Smith Family Foundation, a charity organization that focuses on urban inner-city youths and family support. The foundation has worked with such nonprofit organizations as YouthBuild and the Lupus Foundation of America.

NOTES

1. "Will Smith—Decisions Lead to Destiny." *Orin Woodward Leadership Team.* January 22, 2009. Accessed August 30, 2009. http://orrinwoodward.bloghar bor.com/blog/HistoricalBiographies/_archives/2009/1.

2. "Aishwarya was almost in 'Hitch': director." *IndiaGlitz.* Accessed August 30, 2009. http://www.indiaglitz.com/channels/hindi/interview/6308.html.

3. "Black actors still face Oscar challenges." *CNN.com International*. Accessed August 30, 2009. http://edition.cnn.com/2009/SHOWBIZ/Movies/02/19/black.actors.oscar/index.html#cnnSTCText.

4. Tariq Mohammad, interview with the author, June 27, 2009.

5. "Will Smith on Hollywood, Religion and Tom Cruise." *Newsweek*. Accessed August 30, 2009. http://www.newsweek.com/id/171192.

6. "Will Smith changes direction in Seven Pounds." *News.com.au*. Accessed August 30, 2009. http://www.news.com.au/couriermail/story/0,23739,24865434-7642,00.html.

7. "Fans find a match with Will Smith in 'Hitch'." *CTV.ca—Canadian Television*. Accessed August 30, 2009. http://www.ctv.ca/servlet/ArticleNews/story/CTVNews/1108335473882_24?hub=Entertainment.

8. "Will & Jaden Smith: 'pursuit of HappYness' chronicles the struggles of raising a son and getting ahead: Hollywood's hottest father/son duo." *BNET*. Accessed August 30, 2009. http://findarticles.com/p/articles/mi_m1077/is_3_62/ai_n27101441.

9. "Will Smith Finds Box Office 'Happyness'." *CBS News*. Accessed August 30, 2009. http://www.cbsnews.com/stories/2006/12/17/entertainment/main2274598.shtml?source=RSSattr=HOME_2274598.

10. "Back talk with Chris Gardner." *Free Online Library*. Accessed August 30, 2009. http://www.thefreelibrary.com/Back+talk+with+Chris+Gardner.-a0157033246.

11. "Will & Jaden Smith: 'pursuit of HappYness' chronicles the struggles of raising a son and getting ahead: Hollywood's hottest father/son duo." *BNET*. Accessed August 30, 2009. http://www.accessmylibrary.com/coms2/summary_0286-29014093_ITM.

12. "From Homeless to Hollywood." *ABCNews.com*. Accessed August 30, 2009. http://abcnews.go.com/2020/story?id=2003733&page=1.

13. "The man who inspired Will Smith's new movie." *Chicago Sun-Times*. Accessed August 30, 2009. http://www.suntimes.com/news/metro/174085,CST-NWS-happy15.article.

14. "Smith pushes his range as an actor." *Variety*. Accessed August 30, 2009. http://www.variety.com/article/VR1117997299.html?categoryid=13&cs=1.

15. "Will Smith on Letterman." YouTube video. http://www.youtube.com/watch?v=4qfwIp7BQTY&feature=related.

16. Muccino, Gabriele. "Pursuit of Happyness: Review." *Rolling Stone*. Accessed August 30, 2009. http://www.rollingstone.com/reviews/dvd/7605317/review/12812265/1016_the_pursuit_of_happyness.

17. "Will Smith Interview—The Pursuit of Happyness, Working with Jaden Smith, I Am Legend." *Hollywood Movie News, Upcoming Releases, Interviews, Re-*

views, Photos, and Videos—About.com. Accessed August 30, 2009. http://movies.about.com/od/thepursuitofhappyness/a/pursuitws120806_2.htm.

18. "Jennifer Connelly, Interview, Jaden Smith, Day the Earth Stood Still, Will Smith, Environment, Eco-Friendly, Green." *Star Magazine.* Accessed August 30, 2009. http://www.starmagazine.com/news/14942.

19. "ESPN OTL: Star power on, off field—ESPN Rise FOOTBALL." *ESPN.* Accessed August 30, 2009. http://sports.espn.go.com/highschool/rise/football/news/story?id=3685615&campaign=rsssrch&source=phoenix+coyotes.

20. "Will Smith: My Daughter Wants to Be Paris Hilton—Jaden Smith, Will Smith." *People.com.* Accessed August 30, 2009. http://www.people.com/people/article/0,,20163838,00.html.

21. "Will Smith talks about his continued success." *Herald Sun.* Accessed August 30, 2009. http://www.news.com.au/heraldsun/story/0,21985,22989933-5006023,00.html.

22. Williams, Kam. "Will Smith 'I Am Legend' Interview." *NewsBlaze.* Accessed August 30, 2009. http://newsblaze.com/story/20071218115318toop.nb/topstory.html.

23. "'I Am Legend' Review." *Variety.* Accessed August 30, 2009. http://www.variety.com/review/VE1117935602.html?categoryid=31&cs=1.

24. Williams, Kam. "Will Smith 'I Am Legend' Interview." *NewsBlaze.* Accessed August 30, 2009. http://newsblaze.com/story/20071218115318tsop.nb/topstory.html.

25. *Scientology, What is it?—A Reference from the Church of Scientology.* Accessed August 30, 2009. http://www.whatisscientology.org/

26. "Will Smith defends Tom Cruise, Scientology." *Access Hollywood.* Accessed August 30, 2009. http://www.msnbc.msn.com/id/22088489/

27. "Will Smith Rescues Industry With Explosive Opening For 'I Am Legend'." *ROTTEN TOMATOES.* Accessed August 30, 2009. http://www.rottentomatoes.com/m/i_am_legend/news/1697664/box_office_guru_wrapup_will_smith_rescues_industry_with_explosive_opening_for_i_am_legend.

28. "Will Smith & Jada Pinkett." *Wed TV.* December 31, 1997. Accessed August 30, 2009. http://www.geocities.com/wedtvsite/celeb_willsjadap.html.

29. "Will Smith has found the magic formula." *USATODAY.com.* Accessed August 30, 2009. http://www.usatoday.com/life/movies/news/2008-06-26-will-smith_N.htm.

30. *The Home of Hip Hop Culture and Rap Music.* Accessed August 30, 2009. http://hiphop-blingbling.blogspot.com/feeds/posts/default.

31. "Superhero as superlush: Will Smith's bizarre 'Hancock' goes off-course." *James Sanford At The Movies—MLive.com.* Accessed August 30, 2009. http://blog.mlive.com/james_sanford/2008/07/superhero_as_superlush_will_sm.html.

32. Mccafferty, Dennis. "Will Smith." *USA WEEKEND Magazine*. Accessed August 30, 2009. http://www.usaweekend.com/08_issues/081214/081214will-smith.html.

33. "Love story Seven Pounds terrifies Smith." *Adelaide Now*. Accessed August 30, 2009. http://www.news.com.au/adelaidenow/story/0,22606,24883482-5006346,00.html.

34. "Will Smith accedes to dark role—Seven Pounds." *Cherry Creek News*. Accessed August 30, 2009. http://www.thecherrycreeknews.com/content/view/3745/2/

35. "Will Smith tells his own stories." *Newsobserver.com*. Accessed August 30, 2009. http://www.newsobserver.com/105/story/1339307.html.

36. "Will Smith's hugs, pats were comforting on sets: Woody Harrelson." *Indians in Thailand*. Accessed August 30, 2009. http://www.thaindian.com/news portal/uncategorized/will-smiths-hugs-pats-were-comforting-on-sets-woody-harrelson_100148239.html.

37. "Will Smith on Hollywood, Religion and Tom Cruise." *Newsweek*. Accessed August 30, 2009. http://www.newsweek.com/id/171192.

38. "Rosario Dawson: Will Smith's Leading Lady." *VIBE Magazine*. Accessed August 30, 2009. http://www.vibe.com/news/online_exclusives/2008/12/rosario_dawson_will_smith_leading_lady/.

39. "Jade Behind Will Smith's Love Scenes." *One India*. Accessed August 30, 2009. http://living.oneindia.in/insync/2009/jada-pinkett-smith-will-smith-love making-100109.html.

40. "Will Smith." *USA WEEKEND Magazine*. Accessed August 30, 2009. http://www.usaweekend.com/08_issues/081214/081214will-smith.html>.

41. "Good Will Touring." *The NOssip*. Accessed August 30, 2009. http://www.thenossip.com/2008/12/17/good-will-touring/

42. "Smith using acting to make difference." *UPI.com*. Accessed August 30, 2009. http://www.upi.com/Entertainment_News/2008/12/14/Smith_using_acting_to_make_difference/UPI-38091229282725/

43. "Jaden Smith Gets Acting Tips from Mom and Dad." *People.com*. Accessed August 30, 2009. http://www.people.com/people/article/0,,20245393,00.html.

44. "Will Smith on Hollywood, Religion and Tom Cruise." *Newsweek*. Accessed August 30, 2009. http://www.newsweek.com/id/171192.

45. Tariq Mohammad, interview with the author, June 29, 2009.

46. "Questions About Study Technology." *New Village Leadership Academy*. http://www.nvlacademy.org/news/newsItem.cfm?cms_news_id=24.

47. "Will Smith: Attacks on Tom Cruise Were 'Painful for Me to See'." *The Insider*. Accessed August 30, 2009. http://www.theinsider.com/news/1007954_Will_Smith_Attacks_on_Tom_Cruise_Were_Painful_for_Me_to_See.

48. "Will Smith has found the magic formula." *USATODAY.com.* Accessed August 30, 2009. http://www.usatoday.com/life/movies/news/2008-06-26-will-smith_N.htm.

49. "Will Smith on Hollywood, Religion and Tom Cruise." *Newsweek.* Accessed August 30, 2009. http://www.newsweek.com/id/171192/page/2.

Chapter 7

HELLO, MR. PRESIDENT

There is no pain worse than not achieving a dream when it is your fault.
If God did not want you to have it, that is one thing. But if you do not get
what you desire because you are lazy, there is no pain worse than that.

—*Will Smith*

When Will Smith was a little boy growing up in the 1960s, men such
as Martin Luther King Jr. and Malcolm X were fighting for the equal
rights of fellow African Americans. They fought for the right of blacks
to earn the same pay as whites and the rights to have the same opportunities as everyone else. They wanted the right to dream big and
achieve their dreams. On August 28, 1963, Martin Luther King stood at
the Lincoln Memorial in Washington, D.C., and gave his famed "I have
a dream" speech, in which he said, "I have a dream that one day this
nation will rise up and live out the true meaning of its creed: 'We hold
these truths to be self-evident, that all men are created equal.'"

Throughout Will's career, he made several references in interviews to
the fact that he had the ability to do whatever he set his mind to and
that he had the drive and dedication to succeed. Will was living what
Martin Luther King Jr. and Malcolm X had fought for. Will also read

motivational books, such as *The Alchemist,* which encouraged him to push toward superstardom.

Will also once compared his drive and dedication to getting on the treadmill against someone else in a competition to see who could last the longest. Will explained that there were only two ways he would get off the treadmill—the other person would have to get off the treadmill first, or Will would die on it.

It was this drive and dedication that got Will to where he was at in his career. He knew what it was like for a black man to achieve great-ness—he had seen the likes of Muhammad Ali and Christopher Gardner do it—and had done it himself. But it was another black man's accom-plishment that would make Will cry and almost bring him to his knees.

It was 2005 and one of the five deadliest hurricanes in the history of the United States had struck the New Orleans, Louisiana, area. Hurricane Katrina slammed into the area and caused severe damage, including a storm surge that flooded the levee system. The levee system then broke and flooded 80 percent of the city. Tragically, more than 1,800 people lost their lives.

Will and Jada, eager to do whatever they could to help, traveled to the area to offer assistance with clean up and repairs. It was there that they met Senator Barack Hussein Obama II, an African American who was a junior U.S. Senator from Illinois. Obama was also lending his support and resources. At the time, there was no discussion that Barack Obama would be a candidate in the next presidential race. After all, he had only been sworn in as a senator several months earlier.

Within the next two years, however, the political circuit had changed, and the buzz had started about the good work that Obama was doing. Talk show host Oprah Winfrey touted Obama's potential on her show when she had him as a guest in 2007. On February 10, 2007, Barack Obama announced his candidacy for the president of the United States while standing on the steps of the Old Capitol Building in Spring-field, Illinois. The opportunity to have the first African American presi-dent of the United States had arrived. Will threw his support completely behind Obama, who was only the second political figure that Will had ever supported. The first was Nelson Mandela, the first president of South Africa.

Will not only supported Nelson Mandela, but also helped to celebrate the president's 90th birthday. He was also asked by Mandela to travel to George, South Africa, and host an all-star fund-raising concert. The concert raised more than $1.6 million for Mandela's 46664 AIDS and HIV Awareness Fund. "I have made movies and music," Will told the crowd of 20,000 people about accepting Mandela's invitation to participate. "I felt like that's not enough. I want to fight and I want to struggle."[1]

Will never knew what it was like to struggle the way his ancestors—and even his own parents—had to, but it didn't mean that he couldn't use his resources to help change the future. Americans respected Will as an actor, but the question would soon become, would they listen to what he had to say when it came to the presidency?

In the 2008 presidential race, Barack Obama squared off against New York's Democratic senator, Hillary Rodham Clinton. The race was close at the beginning, but Obama slowly started to gain steam and pull ahead over the next few months. Barack Obama ended up with significantly more donations and support than Clinton. Will and Jada gave their financial support to Obama as well. They power couple had seen something in the Illinois senator when they worked together in Louisiana that they believed would make him a wonderful president.

". . . And that's because I believe what he believes in. I travel around the world a lot, and I was kind of used to people being happy when the Americans showed up. That sort of changed over the last eight years," said Will. "So I'm excited about the new possibilities of hope and change that Barack is bringing."[2]

Obama campaigned successfully and became the Democratic nominee for president; he then went on to face the Republican nominee, John McCain. In November 2008, Will, Jada, Jaden, Willow, and Trey gathered around their television to watch the results of the historic election. Obama won the election and become the 44th president of the United States and the first African American to hold that office.

On January 20, 2009, Barack Obama was sworn in as president. It was one of those extraordinary moments in Will's life that brought the action hero to tears: "With my kids it was no big deal, whereas for myself and for (my wife) Jada, and even more so for our parents, who lived through the struggle for equality, it was so huge, but for our kids the world is different."[3]

When he discussed the whole event on the *Oprah* show the next day, his eyes would start welling up just thinking about the whole experience. He jokingly told Oprah, "Oprah I'm an action hero, I can't be crying on your show," and he proceeded to imitate himself rolling on the floor, sobbing because he was so happy.[4]

Will bears an uncanny resemblance to the new president—especially around the ears—and he has expressed a strong interest in portraying Obama in a future movie. This opportunity for Will to portray President Barack Obama in a biographical movie, *A Man, a Dream*, has been rumored, although there hasn't been much written about it yet. The feature is said to have a $150 million budget and currently doesn't have a release date.

"If I am ordered by my commander-in-chief to star in a film about him, I will do my duty as an American," he said, beaming.[5] One online gossip site has told the story that Will was mistaken for the president one day by an older couple who said, "We love what you're doing. You're so great for the country!"[6]

LOOKING TOWARD THE FUTURE

Making movies is just a part of what I want to build, [to communicate] ideas of hope and inspiration and love and all those things I see in this grand, big picture. So I don't randomly choose work.

—*Will Smith*

It's been almost 12 years since Will and Jada tied the knot and started a family—which is considered a lifetime when it comes to show business relationships—and life has been very good since then. Not many celebrity couples make it half as long as they have, but Will and Jada understand that a successful marriage takes commitment, sacrifice and, what Jada has called, "respectful communication."[7]

Jada said, "We study with one another to see the core of the issue, uproot it, dissect it and handle it." Will adds, "There is no such thing as a real disagreement—only misunderstandings. Very rarely do we argue, because we believe we can get to the bottom of [any misunderstanding]."[8]

When it comes to sacrificing for each other, Jada understands the success that her husband has had and how that relates to her own successful career: "One of the reasons I don't do a lot of the movies that I could do or could star in is that I need to be close to my family. My family needs me, especially my husband. He needs me."

But Will is there for Jada, too, who has had a steady movie career, although not on the same level that Will has had. Jada's last movie, *The Women,* in 2008 was considered a huge success. It was an updated version of the 1939 film, directed by George Cukor, of the same name and made more than $48 million in box-office receipts. Jada portrayed Alex Fisher, a lesbian. Jada loved the part and said she wanted to do more with the lesbian aspect of the role, but the top brass wouldn't let her. It's a controversial statement for a woman married to a man who has been named *People's* Sexiest Man, but Jada loves sparking controversy: "It's always a beautiful thing. You always want to move outside the box, and any time that you do that is going to be controversial. I love controversy. I try to stay in controversy as much as I can, without having my husband's head pop off."[9]

However, when you are a prominent celebrity and you say something controversial, it has a tendency to create problems. When you're a high-profile couple in the limelight as much as Jada and Will are, it is bound to lead to having rumors spread about you, your family, and your private lifestyle. First, the couple dealt with several years of questions about whether they practiced Scientology. Although they have denied that they are Scientologists, it seems that they have incorporated several aspects of the religion into their lives and into the new school they founded in California.

For years, there have also been rumors about the intimate details of their marriage—including the openness of the marriage and their individual sexuality. They have tried to put the rumors to rest, which works for a little while, until the rumors start circulating again. "I don't have an open marriage and no, we're not gay—and you don't trust that?" says Will. "Well then there's nothing that I really have to say to anybody about anything, because at the end of the day, I'm living my life, and I'm happy."[10]

Will and Jada are a truly happy, successful couple who don't seem to have let success go to their heads. When you listen to Will in interviews, he's always talking about how happy he is and that he hasn't changed throughout the years. Even when Will lost his millions, he was truly humbled by the experience. He has said that he knows that money, no matter how much, doesn't make a person: "Money doesn't change people—but money accentuates who and what you are. If you are good, then money makes you better. If you are an asshole, you will be an even bigger asshole!"[11]

The couple has three wonderful children, who are getting a bit older and starting to make their own way in Hollywood. Will and Jada are very focused and dedicated parents and are helping their children achieve their dreams, just as their parents helped them achieve theirs.

It was in 1984 that the martial arts film *The Karate Kid* took the movie industry by storm. Starring Ralph Macchio, Pat Morita, and Elisabeth Shue, it told the story of a young boy who was the underdog in a karate tournament. The inspirational film took in more than $90 million in box-office receipts, earned Pat Morita an Academy Award nomination for Best Supporting Actor, and made millions in sales of *Karate Kid* memorabilia. It was followed up with the sequels *Karate Kid II* and *Karate Kid III*.

In 2008, Will announced that it would be his son, Jaden, who would star as the lead in the next *Karate Kid* film. Veteran action-star Jackie Chan would play the part of the mentor, originally played by Pat Morita, and Jada would also appear in the film. It was Will who understood that the original *Karate Kid* film had a huge following, and in his typical way, he turned to an expert, the original Karate Kid, Ralph Macchio, for help. At one point, Macchio had expressed his concern to the media about the remake being used solely as a platform for Will's son. He also expressed concern that no one, not even veteran comedic actor Jackie Chan, could replace the legendary Pat Morita. After hearing his concerns, Will called and explained to Macchio that he wanted to find his own angle in the film, but wanted to keep true to the original film as well.

Although Will and Jada had to start from the bottom of the Hollywood acting rung and work their way up in the industry, Willow and Jaden have opportunities that might not have otherwise been available to them. Will and Jada may not be stage parents, but they do help to guide their children's careers, choosing the right projects for them. Will and Jada expect that their children will earn the parts, however, and not just have parts handed to them because of who their parents are.

Willow and Jaden are also set to star in the upcoming Warner Bros. feature *Amulet*, an adaptation of the Scholastic graphic novel from Kazu Kibuishi. In *Amulet*, a brother and sister move in with their great-grandfather after the death of their father. The kids have to use the great-grandfather's magic amulet to rescue their mom from a beast that dwells underground. Will has signed on to produce the movie through his Overbrook Entertainment company.

As the kids have gotten older, Jada has not only continued to oversee their acting careers, but has also focused on returning to her own acting career. In 2009, she returned to cable television with a new show on TNT, *Time Heals*, which is set at Richmond Trinity Hospital in North Carolina. *Hawthorne* comes to TNT from Sony Pictures Television in association with Jada's 100% Women Productions, and Jada serves as an executive producer.

Jada plays the role of Christina Hawthorne, a single mother who is also the director of nursing and who takes on just about everyone that stands in her way. Hawthorne is a compassionate and headstrong chief nursing officer heading up a group of dedicated nurses at Richmond Trinity Hospital who spend long days and nights on the hospital's front lines. She is the kind of nurse you want on your side when you or some-one you love is in the hospital. She is the kind of nurse who fights for her patients and doesn't let them slip through the cracks. When nec-essary, she takes on doctors and administrators who are overworked, distracted, or just unable to see the human being behind the hospital chart.

Like Hawthorne, Will and Jada don't let anything stand in their way either. Looking toward the future, Will is still expanding his busi-ness ventures. He is not only a smart actor, but he is also an extremely smart businessman. He recognizes the fact that his success today could be over tomorrow if his audiences decide they are tired of his movies. So he works hard to prepare for the day when he'll have to hang up his acting shingle and pass the torch to the next movie action hero. Or he could take a page out of veteran actor Harrison Ford's book, who re-leased the next episode of *Indiana Jones*, *The Kingdom of the Crystal Skull*, in 2008 when he was 66 years old. It's just a matter of time to see if

Will decides to continue acting or decides to take a step back and try some new ventures, perhaps as producer or director.

Will already has his hand in many activities that could provide a respite from acting if he so desires. Overbrook Entertainment has been busy producing movies such as the upcoming *Amulet*, but the company has also been involved in other ventures. In 2008, Overbrook Entertainment helped a popular online Web site called JibJab close a $7.5 million deal to stay in business. In the music industry, Will also owns a recording studio, called the Boom-Boom Room, in Burbank, California.

Whatever the future has in store for Will, it will, no doubt, be big done Big Willie Style.

CONCLUSION

When a teacher successfully teaches a student, that teacher can be happy about having done their job well. When the student teaches the teacher, the teacher is even more amazed. In Will Smith's life, he has absolutely amazed his acting coach, Aaron Speiser.

"I'm amazed because Will taught me about how much he desires to be the best actor," said Speiser. "To be the biggest and the best are two different issues and he has the desires to be both. He is clear on what he wants and no one works harder. If I had more students like Will Smith. I'd be very fortunate."[12]

Jason Kaufmann, editor of PopEater.com, has said that Will Smith is the real king of all media. "He's dominated in music, movie and TV, and nobody has taken a show or ruled the charts the way that he has," said Kaufmann. "Elvis didn't do it that much in terms of TV. I think that just he has drive, unmatched right now and he knows who he is and also knows people respond to him because he enjoys living. Crowds respond to him and critics respond to him too. You are seeing on the screen the personality that makes him a winning figure all across the medias."[13]

It's hard to find something to dislike about Will Smith. If someone really wanted to put his life under a microscope and examine—*really examine*—it, they might criticize the only thing that tabloids have criticized, and that is his connection to Tom Cruise and to Scientology. Other critics might say that Will really wasn't a superstar until he hit the movie screen and that his songs really weren't true rap songs, no matter how funny or entertaining a package they were wrapped up in. Those who have studied dramatic acting for years might say that Will is simply a Hollywood special-effects cash machine. Those who look at the movies he's done that are more dramatic and have fewer special effects might say that if he were judged by the earnings of those movies alone, he wouldn't be such a megastar.

Those are all valid possible arguments to arrive at when dissecting Will's career, if you're really looking to find something negative.

On the flip side, there is no denying the fact that Will brings in the bucks for Hollywood, and there is no denying that he's been one of the most successful commercial rap artists ever. Over the years, he's grown from a young rapper to a Grammy Award–winning artist. He's grown from a novice comedic actor who once mouthed everyone else's words on the set to a double Academy Award nominee. He's grown from a young kid from Philly to an accomplished, well-respected Hollywood icon. He's grown from a high school graduate, who gave up the path to a college education, to a self-made man who believes that everything is out there to study and learn. He has grown from being a spendthrift millionaire rapper who lost a fortune to earning it back again through nonstop hard work. Along the way, he has shattered more Hollywood records than any other actor. He has also opened doors for other African American rappers and actors.

Will Smith has indeed been at the top of just about every Hollywood movie chart there is and is now one of the richest men in Hollywood. "I think of the universe as this big, master computer," he said. "The keyboard is inside each of us. I have a keyboard inside of me. I just have to figure out what to type, learn the code, to make the things happen that I want."[14] He set out to become the biggest star in the world, and he's achieved that goal, just like he said he would do.

NOTES

1. "Nelson Mandela holds AIDS benefit concert in South Africa; raises $1.6 million." *Jet.* April 11, 2005. Accessed August 30, 2009. http://findarticles.com/p/articles/mi_m1355/is_15_107/ai_n13611427/.

2. "Will Smith gives backing to Obama." *BBC NEWS.* Accessed August 30, 2009. http://news.bbc.co.uk/1/hi/entertainment/7474836.stm.

3. "Will Smith believes Obama will 'change the world forever'." *Entertainment & Showbiz*. Accessed August 30, 2009. http://www.entertainmentand showbiz.com/will-smith-will-smith-believes-obama-will-change-the-world-forever-200901219787.

4. "Will Smith's Obama Happiness, Sobs." [Video.] *The Huffington Post*. Accessed August 30, 2009. http://www.huffingtonpost.com/2008/11/06/will-smiths-obama-happine_n_142003.html.

5. "Will Smith On Obama Role: 'If Ordered . . . I Will Do My Duty As An American'." *The Huffington Post*. Accessed August 30, 2009. http://www.huffing tonpost.com/2009/01/15/will-smith-on-obama-role_n_158113.html.

6. "Will Smith—I'm No Barack!" *TMZ.com*. Accessed August 30, 2009. http://www.tmz.com/2007/02/06/will-smith-im-no-barack.

7. Keith, Amy Elisa. "Jada Pinkett Smith—Her Turn." *People.com*. April 2, 2007. Accessed August 30, 2009. http://www.people.com/people/archive/arti cle/0,,20061745,00.html.

8. Keith, Amy Elisa. "Jada Pinkett Smith—Her Turn." People.com. April 2, 2007. Accessed August 30, 2009. http://www.people.com/people/archive/arti cle/0,,20061745,00.html.

9. "Why Jada is mad about the films and Will, too." *Independent.ie*. Accessed August 30, 2009. http://www.independent.ie/entertainment/film-cinema/why-jada-is-mad-about-the-films-and-will-too-1558223.html.

10. Frazier, John. "Jada Pinkett Smith On Gay and Open Marriage Rumors." *GBMNews*. March 28, 2009. Accessed August 30, 2009. http://www.gbmnews. com/articles/4234/1/Jada-Pinkett-Smith-On-Gay-and-Open-Marriage-Rumors/Page1.html.

11. "Film star actor Will Smith talks to BILD: 'Marriage is more than just sex and cooking!'" *Bild.de*. Accessed August 30, 2009. http://www.bild.de/BILD/ news/bild-english/celebrity-gossip/2009/01/08/film-star-actor-will-smith/visit-to-berlin-marriage-is-more-than-sex-and-cooking.html #

12. Aaron Speiser, interview with the author, June 27, 2009.

13. Jason Kaufmann, interview with the author, June 27, 2009.

14. "Will Smith has found the magic formula." *USATODAY.com*. Accessed August 30, 2009. http://www.usatoday.com/life/movies/news/2008-06-26-will-smith_N.htm.

APPENDIX: LIST OF FILMS AND OTHER WORKS

ACTOR

The Fresh Prince of Bel-Air (1990–1996) as William "Will" Smith
Where the Day Takes You (1992) as Manny
Made in America (1993) as Tea Cake Walters
Six Degrees of Separation (1993) as Paul
Bad Boys (1995) as Mike Lowrey
Independence Day (1996) as Captain Steven Hiller
Men in Black (1997) as James "Agent J" Edwards
Enemy of the State (1998) as Robert Clayton Dean
Wild, Wild West (1998) as Captain James West
The Legend of Bagger Vance (2000) as Bagger Vance
Ali (2001) as Cassius Clay/Cassius X/Muhammad Ali
Men in Black II (2002) as Agent J
Bad Boys II (2003) as Detective Mike Lowery
All of Us (2003–2004) as Johnny [3 episodes]
I, Robot (2004) as Del Spooner
Shark Tale (2004) as Oscar [voice-over]
Hitch (2005) as Alex "Hitch" Hitchens

The Pursuit of Happyness (2006) as Chris Gardner
I Am Legend (2007) as Robert Neville
Hancock (2008) as John Hancock
Seven Pounds (2008) as Ben Thomas

PRODUCER

The Fresh Prince of Bel-Air (1994–1996) [executive producer, 24 episodes]
Showtime (2002) [executive producer]
Ride or Die (2003) [executive producer]
All of Us (2003–2007) [executive producer, 44 episodes]
I, Robot (2004) [executive producer]
The Seat Filler (2004) [executive producer]
Saving Face (2004) [producer]
Hitch (2005) [producer]
ATL (2006) [producer]
The Pursuit of Happyness (2006) [producer]
Hancock (2008) [producer]
The Secret Life of Bees (2008) [producer]
The Human Contract (2008) [executive producer]
Lakeview Terrace (2008) producer]
Seven Pounds (2008) [producer]
Untitled *Karate Kid* remake (2010) [producer]
Pursuit (2010) [producer]
Monster Hunter (2010) [producer]

ALBUMS

DJ Jazzy Jeff and the Fresh Prince

Rock the House—Word-Up, Jive/Zomba 1987
He's the DJ, I'm the Rapper—Jive/Zomba 1988
And in This Corner . . . —Jive/Zomba 1989
Homebase—Jive/Zomba 1991
Code Red—Jive/Zomba 1993
Greatest Hits—Jive 1998
Before the Willennium—BMG 2000
Platinum & Gold Collection—Jive 2003

Solo Albums

Big Willie Style—Sony 1997
Willenium—Sony 1999
Greatest Hits—Sony 2002
Born to Reign—Sony 2002
Lost and Found—Interscope 2005

FILM AND MUSIC

The Fresh Prince of Bel-Air: composed title song
In the Heat of the Night (1989): performed "He's The DJ, I'm The Rapper"
Dr. Demento 20th Anniversary Collection (1991): wrote "Girls Ain't Nothin' but Trouble"
Made in America (1993): wrote and performed "Dance or Die"
Strange Days (1995): wrote and performed "Lost in the Night"
Men in Black (1997): wrote and performed "Men in Black"
Ride (1998): On soundtrack with "Brand New Funk"
The Parent Trap (1998): wrote "Parents Just Don't Understand"
Austin Powers: The Spy Who Shagged Me (1999): on the soundtrack with "Just the Two of Us (Dr. Evil Mix)"
Wild, Wild West (1999): wrote and performed "Wild, Wild West"
Men in Black II (2002): wrote, produced, and performed "Black Suits Comin' (Nod Ya Head)"
Malibu's Most Wanted (2003): wrote and performed "Parents Just Don't Understand"
Jersey Girl (2004): wrote and performed "Parents Just Don't Understand"
Shark Tale (2004): performed "Gotta Be Real"
I Am Legend (2007): performed "I Shot the Sheriff"

AWARDS

2009

Image Award: won, Outstanding Actor in a Motion Picture for *Seven Pounds*
People's Choice Award: won, Favorite Male Movie Star
People's Choice Award: nominated, Favorite Superhero for *Hancock*

2008

Image Award: nominated, Outstanding Actor in a Motion Picture
for *I Am Legend*

MTV Movie Award: won, Best Male Performance for *I Am Legend*

Saturn Award: won, Best Actor for *I Am Legend*

National Movie Award: nominated, Best Performance—Male for
Hancock and also for *I Am Legend*

Teen Choice Award: won, Choice Movie Actor: Horror/Thriller
for *I Am Legend*

Screen Actors Guild Awards: nominated, Outstanding Performance
by a Male Actor in a Leading Role for *The Pursuit of Happyness*

MTV Movie Award: nominated, Best Performance for *The Pursuit
of Happyness*

Askmen.com: nominated for top 49 most influential men of 2008
readers' poll (the top 49 is used to determine who had biggest
impact on the way other men dress, talk, buy, and think over the
past 12 months)

2007

Image Award: nominated, Outstanding Actor in a Motion Picture
for *The Pursuit of Happyness*

Academy Award: nominated, Best Performance by an Actor in a
Leading Role for *The Pursuit of Happyness*

Black Reel: nominated, Best Actor for *The Pursuit of Happyness*

Black Reel: nominated, Best Film for *The Pursuit of Happyness*

Critics Choice Award: nominated, Best Actor for *The Pursuit of
Happyness*

Golden Globe: nominated, Best Performance by an Actor in a Motion Picture—Drama for *The Pursuit of Happyness*

Blimp Award: nominated, Favorite Male Movie Star for *The Pursuit
of Happyness*

NRJ Ciné Award: won, International Star of the Year for *The Pursuit of Happyness*

TV Land Award: nominated, Little Screen/Big Screen Star

Teen Choice Award: won, Choice Movie Actor: Drama (2006) for
The Pursuit of Happyness

Teen Choice Award: won, Choice Movie: Chemistry (2006) for
The Pursuit of Happyness

2006

People's Choice Award: nominated, Favorite Funny Male Star

Blimp Award: won, Favorite Movie Actor for *Hitch*

Image Award: nominated, Outstanding Actor in a Motion Picture
for *Hitch*

Black Reel: nominated, Best Actor for *Hitch*

Black Movie Award: nominated, Outstanding Motion Picture for
ATL

CFCA Award: nominated, Best Actor for *The Pursuit of Happyness*

TV Land Award: nominated, Little Screen/Big Screen Star (Men)

2005

Teen Choice Award: won, Choice Movie Actor: Comedy for *Hitch*

Teen Choice Award: nominated, Choice Movie Blush Scene for
Hitch

Teen Choice Award: nominated, Choice Movie Dance Scene for
Hitch

Teen Choice Award: nominated, Choice Movie Liplock for *Hitch*

Teen Choice Award: nominated, Choice Movie Love Scene for
Hitch

Teen Choice Award: nominated, Choice Movie Rockstar Moment
for *Hitch*

People's Choice Award: won, Favorite Male Action Movie Star

MTV Movie Award: nominated, Best Comedic Performance for
Hitch

MTV Movie Award: nominated, Best Male Performance for *Hitch*

Image Award: nominated, Outstanding Actor in a Motion Picture
for *I, Robot*

Blimp Award: won, Favorite Voice from an Animated Movie for
Shark Tale

BET Comedy Award: nominated, Best Performance in an Animated Theatrical Film for *Shark Tale*

Honorary César Award in France

BET Comedy Award: nominated, Outstanding Lead Actor in a
   Theatrical Film for *Hitch*
Black Movie Award: nominated, Outstanding Performance by an
   Actor in a Leading Role for *Hitch*
TV Land Award: nominated, Little Screen/Big Screen Star

2004

MTV Movie Award: nominated, Best On-Screen Team for *Bad
   Boys II*
Image Award: nominated, Outstanding Actor in a Motion Picture
   for *Bad Boys II*
TV Land Award: nominated, Favorite "Fish Out of Water" for *The
   Fresh Prince of Bel-Air*

2003

Blimp Award: nominated, Favorite Movie Actor for *Men in Black II*
Kid's Choice Awards: Wannabe Award. The Wannabe Award is
   presented to the celebrity role model or inspiration or the person
   whom the kids want to be like.
TV Land Award: nominated, Small Screen to Silver Screen
VES Award: nominated, Best Performance by an Actor in an Effects Film for *Men in Black II*

2002

ShoWest Award: Male Star of the Year
MTV Movie Award: won, Best Male Performance for *Ali*
BET Award: won, Best Actor
Image Award: nominated, Outstanding Actor in a Motion Picture
   for *Ali*
Golden Globe: nominated, Best Performance by an Actor in a Mo-
   tion Picture—Drama for *Ali*
Black Reel: nominated, Theatrical—Best Actor for *Ali*
Critics Choice Award: nominated, Best Actor for *Ali*
Academy Award: nominated, Best Actor in a Leading Role for *Ali*
Teen Choice Award: nominated, Film—Choice Actor, Drama
   Action/Adventure for *Men in Black II*

2001

Image Award: nominated, Outstanding Actor in a Motion Picture for *The Legend of Bagger Vance*

Saturn Award: nominated, Best Supporting Actor for *The Legend of Bagger Vance*

Blockbuster Entertainment Award: nominated, Favorite Actor—Drama/Romance for *The Legend of Bagger Vance*

2000

Razzie Award: won, Worst Original Song for *Wild, Wild West* [Song: "Wild, Wild West"]

Razzie Award: won, Worst Screen Couple for *Wild, Wild West*

ASCAP Award: won, Most Performed Songs from Motion Pictures for *Wild, Wild West*

Blimp Award: won, Favorite Song from a Movie for *Wild, Wild West* [Song: "Wild, Wild West"]

Blimp Award: nominated, Favorite Movie Actor for *Wild, Wild West*

Blockbuster Entertainment Award: nominated, Favorite Action Team for *Wild, Wild West*

Blockbuster Entertainment Award: nominated, Favorite Song from a Movie for *Wild, Wild West* [Song: "Wild, Wild West"]

1999

ShoWest Award: Actor of the Year

MTV Movie Award: nominated, Best Male Performance for *Enemy of the State*

Image Award: nominated, Outstanding Lead Actor in a Motion Picture for *Enemy of the State*

Special Award: Entertainer of the Year

Blockbuster Entertainment Award: won, Favorite Actor—Action/Adventure for *Enemy of the State*

1998

Teen Choice Award: nominated, Film—Choice Actor for *Enemy of the State*

MTV Movie Award: won, Best Fight for *Men in Black*

MTV Movie Award: won, Best Movie Song for *Men in Black* [Song: "Men in Black"]

MTV Movie Award: nominated, Best Comedic Performance for *Men in Black*

MTV Movie Award: nominated, Best On-Screen Duo for *Men in Black*

Blockbuster Entertainment Award: won, Favorite Actor—Science Fiction for *Men in Black*

Blimp Award: won, Favorite Movie Actor for *Men in Black*

ASCAP Award: won, Most Performed Songs from Motion Pictures for *Men in Black*

Saturn Award: nominated, Best Actor—Science Fiction for *Men in Black*

1997

Special Award: International Box Office Achievement

MTV Movie Award: won, Best Kiss for *Independence Day*

MTV Movie Award: nominated, Best Male Performance for *Independence Day*

Image Award: nominated, Outstanding Lead Actor in a Comedy Series for *The Fresh Prince of Bel-Air*

Blockbuster Entertainment Award: won, Favorite Actor—Science Fiction for *Independence Day*

Saturn Award: nominated, Best Actor for Independence Day

Blimp Award: nominated, Favorite Movie Actor for *Independence Day*

Kid's Choice Awards Hall of Fame

1996

MTV Movie Award: nominated, Best On-Screen Duo for *Bad Boys*

Image Award: nominated, Outstanding Lead Actor in a Comedy Series for *The Fresh Prince of Bel-Air*

Blimp Award: nominated, Favorite Television Actor for *The Fresh Prince of Bel-Air*

Universe Reader's Choice Award: won, Best Actor in a Genre Motion Picture for *Independence Day*

1995

ShoWest Award: Male Star of Tomorrow

1994

Golden Globe: won, Top TV Series for *The Fresh Prince of Bel-Air*
Golden Globe: won, Best Performance by an Actor in a TV Series—Comedy/Musical for *The Fresh Prince of Bel-Air*

1993

Golden Globe: nominated, Best Performance by an Actor in a TV Series—Comedy/Musical for *The Fresh Prince of Bel-Air*

1991

Blimp Award: won, Favorite TV Award for *The Fresh Prince of Bel-Air*

FURTHER READING

BOOKS

Berenson, Jan. *Will Power! A Biography of Will Smith*. New York: Simon Spotlight Entertainment, 1997.

Corrigan, Jim. *Will Smith* (Hip Hop). New York: Mason Crest, 2007.

Doeden, Matt. *Will Smith* (Just the Facts Biographies). Minneapolis, MN: Lerner Publications, 2006.

Embacher, Eric. *Will Smith: The Funny, Funky, and Confident Fresh Prince* (High Five Reading). Belmont, MN: Red Brick Learning, 2003.

Smith, W. *Just the Two of Us*. Illustrated by Kadir Nelson. New York: Scholastic Bookshelf, 2005.

ONLINE RESOURCES

Billboard magazine. http://www.billboard.com. Offers full coverage of breaking music news and music chart toppers to music executives and fans alike. *Billboard* is a print and online music magazine for in-depth music business news and access to an array of digital music, business tools, and music videos.

Hollywood Reporter magazine. http://www.Hollywoodreporter.com. A daily trade
    publication.
Rolling Stone. http://www.rollingstone.com. Print and online editions.
TVWeek http://www.tvweek.com. Breaking entertainment television news and
    analysis covering TV ratings, broadcast, cable, syndication, viral video,
    Emmys Awards, and upfronts.

INDEX

About the Author

LISA M. IANNUCCI is the author of *Ellen DeGeneres* (Greenwood, 2009) and has written many other books and magazine articles. She has contributed celebrity articles to BobVila.com and Executive Travel and is the founder of a blog on celebrity do-gooders, http://celebrity-do-gooders.blogspot.com.

She lives in upstate New York and has been a fan of Will Smith's since his early days in rap and on *The Fresh Prince of Bel-Air*.